BIG ENGLISH PLUS 6

Mario Herrera • Christopher Sol Cruz

T0385913

PUPIL'S BOOK

Contents

CLIL/Culture	Writing	Life Skills/Project	Phonics	I can...
Social Science: School days in China average, belief, bright, ceremony, gather, limited, packed, strengthen, study period, timetable, typical **Around the World: An alternative school in Finland** composting, curriculum, focused, memorising, pace, practical, workshop	Opinion paragraph	**Manage your time wisely.** Talk about how you spend your time and how you manage it. Create a graph to see how pupils spend their time.	**spr, str, scr** spring, sprint street, strong screen, screw	...talk about school activities and homework. ...say what I have and haven't done.
Social Science: Amazing young people ability, co-found, compose, determined, exceptional talent, gifted, inspiration, keep in touch, legend, social media, symphony **Additional language:** reflexive pronouns *whom* **Around the World: Seeds of Peace** conflict resolution, critical thinking, journalist, leader, neutral environment, peace	Biography	**Appreciate yourself.** Talk about your amazing qualities and talents. Make an 'Amazing Me' collage and interview classmates about their amazing qualities and talents.	**spl, squ, thr** splash, split squash, squid three, throat	...talk about past experiences. ...talk about amazing people's accomplishments (including my own).
Social Science: Ethics acceptable, according to, based on, ethical, ethics, excuse, harmless, morally, perspective, respectful, traits, treat **Around the World: Proverbs** common sense, consequences, hasty, pass on, proverb, reap, regret, sound advice, sow, weigh up	Story ending	**Do the right thing.** Discuss the right choice to make when faced with a dilemma. Make a class handbook about doing the right thing.	**nch, nth, mpt** crunch, lunch month, tenth prompt, tempt	...talk about consequences and possibilities and give advice. ...talk about doing the right thing.
Science and Technology: Predictions for the future: Experts arena, be applied to, futurist, imaginary, interact with, microscopic, nanotechnology, revolutionise, treat, virtual reality, wireless, 3-D **Around the World: Predictions for the future: Kids** citizen, co-exist, gender, harmoniously, manual work, religion, shelter, shuttle, time machine, turn out	Formal and informal emails	**Make good decisions.** Talk about how the decisions you make now affect the future. Pupils write letters to themselves in the future and share them with the class.	**/s/, /z/, /iz/** eats, cooks, sleeps runs, sings, swims dances, washes, watches	...talk about and make predictions about the future. ...talk about levels of certainty. ...report actual speech.
Science: Super power or super science? activate, adhesive, electrode, endless, experiment, fascinating, gecko, gesture, interact, skyscraper, spell out, work on **Around the World: Superheroes** android, bolt of lightning, bullet, cape, meteorite, mischievous, mission, originate, reflexes, superhuman, trauma	Character traits	**Take positive steps for the future.** Discuss amazing achievements and things we can do to help the future of the world. Make a class book about positive steps for the future.	**/t/, /d/, /id/** looked, walked, watched called, cleaned, climbed ended, painted, wanted	...talk about what I would, could and might do in different situations. ...answer questions about unreal situations.
Science: Amazing animals and plants absorb, adapt, blink, break down, carnivore, digest, give birth, herbivore, infection, injure, nectar, nutrients, protein, rays, slippery **Around the World: Legacies of ancient civilisations** concept, contribution, cultivation, elections, influence, inspiration, legacy, revolution, terraced farming	From story to play	**Appreciate school.** Complete a chart and discuss practical uses for the topics learnt at school. Create a book of words/names from ancient Greece that are used today.	**er, est** cheaper, easier, faster, happier best, longest	...talk about school subjects and what I learn. ...identify some legacies of ancient civilisations. ...compare things using *more/most, fewer/fewest, less/least*. ...talk about rules and obligations.
Science: Aurora borealis altitude, atmosphere, clapping, interaction, nitrogen, observe, oxygen, phenomenon, pole, solar wind, stand out, swirling **Additional language:** *whose* **Around the World: Mysterious findings** construct, diameter, estimate, evidence, existence, footprint, spherical, ton	Cause and effect	**Be curious.** Learn the importance of fostering one's own curiosity. Create a booklet about two mysteries.	**un, inter, re, pre, super** unhappy international recycle, reduce preused Superman	...discuss mysterious phenomena. ...confirm information using question tags. ...agree using *So/Neither*. ...use compound adjectives.
History: Archeological discoveries archaeologist, artefact, carving, dig, excavate, goddess, mummified, pharaoh, remains, tomb, treasure **Around the World: Seven wonders of the modern world** antiquity, compile, empire, gladiator, Hellenic, honorary, landmark, peninsula, sightseers, structure	Report	**Take pride in your town or city.** Describe special places, monuments or other attractions of one's own town/city or a nearby city. Create a map for a bicycle trip to famous or interesting places in one's town/city.	**able, ful, ly** comfortable, washable beautiful, peaceful deeply, slowly	...talk about famous places and structures around the world. ...describe places and structures using the passive voice, relative clauses and the causative form.
Social Science: The history of video games arcade game, artificial intelligence, coins, compete, electronic device, gamer, games console, industry, intended, invent, multiplayer, shortage **Around the World: Unique musical instruments** bagpipes, concertina, distinctive sound, herdsmen, horn, mellow, note, sitar, steel drums	Film review	**Appreciate different opinions.** Read and discuss the opinions of several young people. Make an opinion map to compare, discuss and record classmates' opinions about a topic.	**sion, tion, ation** decision, television fiction, option celebration, invitation	...talk about entertainment. ...talk about people's opinions. ...report what people say.

ALL ABOUT SCHOOL

1 Read and listen to the statements. All of them are true! Talk about them with a partner. Which one is the most surprising? Why?

1 Some kids have *didaskaleinophobia*, which is a fear of going to school.

2 Richard Branson, creator of *Virgin Records* and the *Virgin Atlantic* airline, didn't finish secondary school.

3 There is an alternative school in Canada that doesn't test pupils and it doesn't follow a strict timetable, either. Pupils decide how to spend the school day and which activities to attend. They are grouped not by their age but by their interests.

4 Finnish pupils rarely take exams or do homework until they are into their teens. But they rank at the top or near the top in international tests in Science, Maths and Language.

5 China's got the longest school day in the world. A Chinese pupil spends almost eleven hours in the classroom each day!

6 In South Korea, secondary school pupils applying for university all take the same standardised test. On the day of the test, people come to the school to support pupils who are going to take the test. They give out sweets, tea and other treats to the pupils. Some taxis give pupils free rides and additional trains and buses run before and after the exam.

2 Read and listen to these bad excuses. Say what each person should have done. Use the phrases in the box.

TIP
Use *should* + *have* + past participle form of the verb to give advice about something in the past.

been more careful   done it earlier
done it again   paid attention to the time
taken it away from her

1 Q: Have you done your homework yet?   She should have ⸮.

  A: No, I haven't…

2 Q: Have you studied for the test yet?   She should have ⸮.

  A: No, I haven't…

3 Q: Have you finished your project yet?   He should have ⸮.

  A: Yes, I have, but…

4 Q: Have you handed in your essay yet?   He should have ⸮.

  A: No, I haven't…

5 Q: Have you done your Maths homework yet?   He should have ⸮.

  A: No, I haven't…

3 Work with a partner. Take turns making up your own bad excuses.

Have you finished your homework yet?

Why not?

No, I haven't.

There was a power cut and I couldn't find my torch.

THINK BIG When do we usually give excuses? What's the difference between an excuse and an explanation?

7

4 Listen and read. What's the problem? What different advice is offered?

www.webforum.com

boy1_xyz

Hey, you guys. I'm only twelve years old and I'm already under so much stress. I think I'm developing didaskaleinophobia. Have you ever had it? It feels like school is one long punishment. I've got so much homework! I've barely got time to talk to my friends! What shall I do?

cookie48

Uh oh. That's not good. Have you told your parents? I told mine about my situation and we ended up having a meeting with my teacher. That might sound stressful but it was actually helpful. My teacher still gives a lot of homework but she helps me manage it. Things aren't perfect but I feel better.

34309843_kc

Take my advice, boy1_xyz: Don't tell your parents! Trust me – they'll think you just don't like studying. You'll end up in more trouble than you were in before.

imsoclever

I agree with cookie48. Tell your parents about your situation and about how it's making you feel. Show them all your homework.

cute_girl28

I disagree with 34309843_kc. I had the same problem. At first, I couldn't tell my parents but then every Sunday, I'd start feeling sick at the thought of going to school the next day. I finally told my parents. They talked to my teachers and it helped. At the end of the school year, I ended up transferring to an alternative school. My new school suits me much better. We've got much more freedom. We choose our subjects and school activities. I've been here for a month now and I'm MUCH happier.

citymouse1

Hey, cute_girl28. Your school sounds reaaaaaally cool! Where is it?

techieboy03

I've already researched alternative schools, citymouse1. There are some great ones in the UK. I've also researched similar schools in Scotland. There are some really cool ones that are unusual and interesting. I'm guessing but I think your school might be in London, cute_girl28. Am I right?

cute_girl28

You're close, techieboy03. Good guess! You're a great detective. There are a lot of alternative schools in London. I know because I researched it, too! My school is in Brighton. I just love my school!

boy1_xyz

I like your idea. I think an alternative school would fix my problem. But those schools are difficult to get into and there are only a few of them.

rainbowgirl

Why not try homeschooling? I'm being homeschooled and I really like it. My mum teaches me all the subjects. We go on field trips a lot. And once a year, we go to an event just for homeschoolers. It's very exciting. I look forward to it every summer!

READING COMPREHENSION

 Read and say yes, no **or** doesn't say.

1 Boy1_xyz has already told his parents about his problem.

2 Cookie48 has spoken to his teacher about his problem.

3 Imsoclever and cookie48 give the same advice.

4 Cute_girl28 lives in Scotland.

5 Techieboy03 likes being at a traditional school.

 THINK BIG Who do you think gave the best advice to boy1_xyz? Why/Why not? What advice would you give to boy1_xyz?

Language in Action

6 Listen and read. What have Peter and his mum already discussed?

Mum: Peter, I'm about to ask you a question. Can you guess what?

Peter: You're about to ask me if you can increase my pocket money.

Mum: Ha ha. Have you finished your homework yet?

Peter: Not exactly. I'm talking to Tessa.

Mum: Yes, I can see that. May I speak to you, please?

Peter: OK. *[to phone]* Tessa, I've got to go. I'll call you back later.

Mum: So you haven't 'exactly' finished your homework yet?

Peter: Yeah, well, I've finished my Maths homework and I've almost finished my English essay but I haven't started my History assignment yet.

Mum: We've been through this before, Peter. Homework first, phone calls later.

Peter: I know. Sorry, Mum. I'll do it now.

7 Practise the dialogue in 6 with a partner.

8 Listen and match. Then complete the sentences. Use the correct form of the verb.

> get his licence   meet the new pupil
> see the music video   walk the dog

1 Mark's brother has already ❓ .

2 Stacey hasn't ❓ yet.

3 Roberto has already ❓ .

4 Dawn hasn't ❓ yet.

Has she **done** her solo <u>yet</u>?	Yes, she **has**. She **has** <u>already</u> **done** it.
	No, she **hasn't**. She **hasn't done** it <u>yet</u>.
Have t̲h̲ey <u>ever</u> **won** an award?	Yes, they **have**./No, they **haven't**.

Tip: Use the present perfect to talk about an event that happened at an indefinite time in the past. The specific time is unknown or unimportant.

9 Make questions and answers. Follow the example.

1 **Q:** you/do/your homework/yet
   Have you done your homework yet?
   A: *Yes, I've already done it.*   **A:** *No, I haven't done it yet.*

2 **Q:** he/finish his project/yet

3 **Q:** they/ever/be on a field trip

4 **Q:** your parents/speak to the teacher/yet

5 **Q:** she/give the book back/yet

| He **has** <u>already</u> **finished** the project. | He **finished** it <u>yesterday</u>. |
| He **hasn't finished** the project <u>yet</u>. | He **didn't finish** it <u>yesterday</u>. |

Tip: Use the present perfect when no specific time is given. Use the past simple when giving a specific time in the past.

10 Look at Jan's to-do list. Then complete the questions about it and answer them. Follow the example.

1 (*talk*) Has Jan *talked to Jenny yet?*
   Yes, she has. She talked to her at 4:00.

2 (*check email*) Has Jan ❓

3 (*start reading*) Has Jan ❓

4 (*write essay*) Has Jan ❓

5 (*finish Science project*) Has Jan ❓

Things to do:

1 Call Jenny at 4:00. ✔

2 Check email at 4:15. ✔

3 Start reading my book. ✘

4 Write essay. ✔

5 Finish Science project. ✘

11 Read and answer with a partner. Check your answers with the class.

    1 How many hours do you spend at school each day?

    2 How many lessons are there?

    3 How much break time is there?

13

12 Listen and read. How many lessons are there in a Chinese school day? How many breaks are there?

> **CONTENT WORDS**
>
> average belief bright ceremony gather limited
> packed strengthen study period timetable typical

A School Day in China

1   It's noon and the bell is ringing at your school. By now, you've probably spent around seven hours there. Maybe you've had five or six lessons, a few short breaks and a longer break of up to an hour for lunch. If you think that's a tough timetable, you might have to think again! A school day in China can be almost eleven hours long – that's three hours longer than the average working day there!

2   Let's take a look at a typical school day in China. School begins at 7:30 with a flag-raising ceremony and a speech from the head teacher. The first three lessons last from 7:45 to 10:20 with three ten-minute breaks in between. At 10:30, pupils gather at the sports ground to do half an hour of morning exercises. Chinese people believe that keeping fit is important and people of all ages often make time to exercise during the day. Before the fourth lesson begins at 11:25, it's time to do some eye exercises. These exercises usually take five minutes and are for strengthening pupils' eyesight.

3   Lunch is at 12:20 but it's a short break: only twenty minutes. After lunch, there's a study period of one hour, followed by a fifteen-minute break. Then it's back to the classroom for the fifth lesson and some more eye exercises. By then it's 3:40 but the bell hasn't rung yet! There are three more lessons before school finishes at ten past six. What's more, when the school day has ended, pupils can't always go home and relax. Weekday evenings and most of the weekend are often packed with extra lessons and activities such as doing sports, playing a musical instrument or learning another language.

4   As you can see, Chinese pupils work hard and their free time is very limited. All Chinese children learn, from a young age, to be good pupils, get good grades and help other pupils do the same. Behind this tough timetable is the belief that a good education is the key to a bright future.

13 Look at 12. Read and and say true or false.

1 A typical day in a Chinese school is shorter than a typical day in a Chinese office.

2 Every day starts in the same way.

3 Morning exercise is before the third lesson.

4 Pupils do eye exercises because they need to relax.

5 Most pupils in China have got more lessons after school.

6 In China, studying hard is more important than free time and relaxing.

14 Copy the table timetable in your notebook and complete.

Timetable

7:30–7:40 a.m.	flag-raising ceremony		12:50–1:50	study period
7:40–7:45	prepare the classroom		2:00–2:15	6 ?
7:45–8:30	1 ?		2:25–2:30	classroom prep
8:40–9:25	2 ?		2:30–3:15	5th lesson
9:35–10:20	3rd lesson		3:25–3:30	7 ?
10:30–11:00	3 ?		3:40–4:25	8 ?
11:10–11:15	4 ?		4:35–5:20	9 ?
11:25–12:10 p.m.	4th lesson		5:30–6:10	8th lesson or study period
12:20–12:40	5 ?			

15 Work with a partner. Look at the things. Compare your school day and a Chinese school day. Give your opinion.

> a flag-raising ceremony   after-school activities   eye exercises   length of lunch break
> morning exercise   number of breaks   number of lessons and study periods   relaxing

Chinese students do eye exercises, but we don't. Which is better?

I don't think we need eye exercises. Longer breaks are more important.

16 Discuss these questions in groups. Collect ideas, then write about a typical school day in your notebook.

1 What happens on an average school day in your country?

2 What extra lessons or activities do pupils do?

3 How much free time have pupils got? What do they do with it?

17 Listen and read. What has Martha's brother done with her mobile phone?

Tyler:	You look really upset, Martha. Are you OK?
Martha:	Well, no. Have you ever had one of those days where everything goes wrong?
Tyler:	What's happened?
Martha:	My computer has crashed three times today and I've lost my entire Geography project.
Tyler:	Oh no, that's awful!
Martha:	Yeah, but wait, I haven't told you the worst thing yet. My little brother dropped my mobile phone down the toilet this morning.
Tyler:	No! My brother's annoying but he's never done anything that bad.
Martha:	So... now I've lost my phone and all my friends' phone numbers.
Tyler:	You can borrow my old phone if you like.
Martha:	It's OK, thanks. My mum has already lent me one.

18 Look at 17 and complete.

We make the present perfect tense with **have/has** + **past participle**.	My computer ¹ three times today. I ² my entire Geography project. I ³ you the worst thing yet. ⁴ **ever** ⁵ one of those days?
Regular and irregular participles:	**Regular:** played, studied, cra ⁶ , dro ⁷ **Irregular:** eaten, ha ⁸ , lo ⁹ , do ¹⁰
We can use **ever**, **never**, **already** and **yet** with the present perfect tense.	¹¹ one of those days? My brother ¹² anything that bad. My mum ¹³ me a phone. I **haven't told** my dad **yet**.
We can use the present perfect to say **how many times** something has happened.	My computer ¹⁴ today.

19 Read and complete.

1   – studied
2 drink –
3   – had
4 write –

5   – done
6 take –
7   – lost
8 eat –

9   – broken
10 see –
11   – carried
12 be –

20 Read and complete. Use the correct form of the words in the box.

> break her leg   go to Egypt   have a baby   not finish my Spanish homework
> see this film   speak to him   stop working

1   My cousins ⚇ on holiday. They'll be back next week.

2   I ⚇ yet. I'm going to finish it tomorrow.

3   My aunt ⚇! His name's Erol.

4   Lauren ⚇, so she can't walk easily.

5   I ⚇ before. Shall we change the channel?

6   We don't know him well but we ⚇ three or four times.

7   My watch ⚇. It needs a new battery.

21 Read and complete. Use the correct form of the words.

He ¹⚇ (jump) out of burning buildings, he ²⚇ (fall) from high bridges and he ³⚇ (crash) hundreds of cars and motorbikes. He's only thirty-two but he ⁴⚇ (die, already) five times! He ⁵⚇ (be) in more than fifty action films and thrillers but you ⁶⚇ (see, never) his face. Who is he? Meet Craig Haviland, one of Hollywood's top stuntmen. He does all the dangerous things in films that the actors can't do.

Craig, how many times ⁷⚇ *(you, jump) from California's Golden Gate Bridge?*

Actually, I ⁸⚇ (jump, never) off it but I ⁹⚇ (fall) off it three times!

¹⁰⚇ *(you, hurt, ever) yourself?*

Yes, I ¹¹⚇ (have) quite a few accidents. I ¹²⚇ (break) my arm twice and I ¹³⚇ (hurt) my back a few times. But luckily, I ¹⁴⚇ (break, never) a leg. My job is very dangerous but I love it!

22 Think about you, your family and your friends. Choose one interesting thing you/they have done and one interesting thing you/they have never done. Make sentences, then tell the class.

> I've been to Australia.

> I've never ridden a horse.

> My friend Ella has never seen the sea!

A School Day With a Difference

1 "Moi, Sofia!" "Terve, Aleksi!" That's how pupils and teachers say hello to each other at Anna Hansson's school in Finland. Pupils at this school call their teachers by their first names. Anna shouts "Moi" to her friends, too, when she arrives at school at 7:45 in the morning. She has been at the same school since Year 1, so she knows everybody.

2 Anna's school is different from most other schools in Europe. First, Anna and her classmates decide, along with their teacher, what their weekly activities will be. Also, pupils work at their own pace and don't always do the same things. Some may be doing Maths while others might be doing something practical. This month, Anna has practised cooking and making a magazine in different workshops.

23 Look at the statements. Which statements describe your school? Choose and compare with a partner.

1 We memorise a lot of facts. Sometimes that's boring.

2 Sometimes we help to clean the classroom.

3 The breaks are short, so we don't get much exercise.

4 We haven't got much homework, so I've got lots of free time. It's great!

5 There's lots of reading and writing. I'd like to learn something practical instead.

6 We have exams and tests very often, so I have to study a lot.

24 Read the article quickly. Match sentences a–d to paragraphs 1–6.

a Pupils can have bread and a glass of milk, too.

b In Finland, being responsible and helping others is very important.

c They don't follow the same program or do the same activities every week.

d They often work in pairs or groups, then share what they know.

3   Anna and her classmates don't learn by memorising facts. Working together and gathering information is more important in this system. They ask their teacher for help whenever they need it. Pupils are generally very focused and active, so the teacher doesn't often have to tell them to behave.

4   Breaks are an important part of the school day. After a double lesson (90 mins), pupils have a double, 30-minute break. Teachers encourage pupils to go out and get some fresh air even if the weather is bad. Being active makes pupils hungry, so lunchtime is also very popular! At Anna's school, pupils get free hot meals every day. Today's lunch is everybody's favourite – meatballs and mashed potatoes! It's served on tables with tablecloths and flowers in vases.

5   Chores have always been part of the curriculum at Anna's school. They include looking after plants, collecting rubbish, recycling and composting. Pupils also help in the library and in the kitchen.

6   School is over by two o'clock. Most parents work, so in the afternoon there are clubs and hobby groups before pupils go home. Pupils can study Japanese, learn an instrument and do arts and crafts. When Anna gets home in the evening, she's free to do whatever she likes because she hardly ever has any homework!

16

25 **Listen and read. Complete the sentences with phrases from the text.**

1 Anna's school is different from ⁇.

2 Pupils don't always learn the same thing at the same speed. They work ⁇.

3 If they need to, pupils can ⁇ in a lesson.

4 Bad behaviour isn't a problem because pupils are usually ⁇.

5 Pupils ⁇ even if the weather isn't very good.

6 Anna is free to ⁇ after school.

26 **Copy the survey questions in your notebook. Write three more questions, then ask pupils at your school. Collect the results as a class.**

1 I'd like to do fewer subjects than we do now. ☐

   I'd like to do more subjects than we do now. ☐

2 I'd like to have more hours of school every day. ☐

   I'd like to have fewer hours of school every day. ☐

3 We should have more and longer breaks. ☐

   I think we have enough break time. ☐

THINK BIG What are the similarities and what are the differences between your school and Anna's school?

Writing | Opinion paragraph

 27 Read the opinion paragraph about homework.

Homework Does Not Make Pupils Learn Better

Does homework make pupils learn better? In my opinion, it does not. In fact, having a lot of homework makes pupils dislike school and become stressed. Pupils who are anxious and don't like school cannot learn well. Pupils who have got hours and hours of homework cannot relax and spend quality time with their families. I believe that school timetables should allow pupils to get most of their schoolwork done at school. In this way, when they get home, they can be free to enjoy time with their family or just relax. In my opinion, a more relaxed pupil will perform better in class. Too much homework prevents this!

 28 Look at 27 again. Copy and complete the paragraph outline.

Title rewritten as question: ?
Main opinion: ?
Reason: ?
Suggestion: ?
Conclusion: ?

29 Choose one of these school issues or use one of your own ideas and write about it:
- Do you think memorising facts makes pupils learn better?
- Do you think school uniforms should be required?

1 Copy the chart in 28 and complete it with information about your topic.

2 Write your own paragraph.

3 Share it with the class.

30 How do you spend your time? Copy the list of activities and add two more. Tick (✔) the ones you have to do each week and write the number of hours.

Activity	Approximate hours per week
⸮ attend lessons	⸮
⸮ travel to and from school	⸮
⸮ eat	⸮
⸮ sleep	⸮
⸮ study or do homework	⸮
⸮ play sports or exercise	⸮
⸮ participate in school clubs	⸮
⸮ do chores	⸮
⸮ watch TV	⸮
⸮ chat with friends online or by phone	⸮
⸮ ⸮	⸮
⸮ ⸮	⸮

THINK BIG Do you think you manage your time wisely? Do you always have enough time to study, to look after your health, to sleep and to relax? Are the activities you spend the most time doing important? Why/Why not?

PROJECT

31 Make a graph about how you spend your time in a typical school week. Share it with the class.

My graph shows that in a typical week, I spend most of my time at school or studying. But I also spend time with my friends, my family and on the phone and the internet. That's important! I don't spend enough time exercising. I'm going to work on managing my time better!

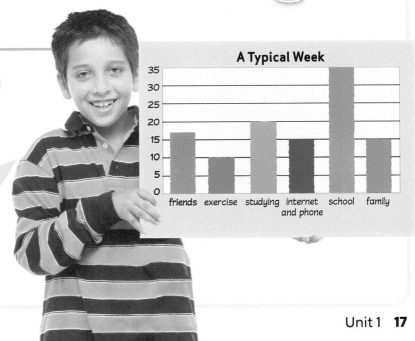

A Typical Week

Listening and Speaking

 32 **Listen, read and repeat.**

1 spr **2** str **3** scr

 33 **Listen and blend the sounds.**

1 spr-i-ng — spring **2** str-ee-t — street

3 scr-ee-n — screen **4** spr-i-n-t — sprint

5 str-o-ng — strong **6** scr-ew — screw

 34 **Listen and chant.**

> I'm fast, I'm strong,
> I can sprint all day long.
> In the spring, in the street,
> Greeting people that I meet!

35 Look at the list of school activities and think of some really bad excuses for why you haven't done these things yet. Work in a group. Ask and answer questions.

complete your research project   do your homework   join any after-school clubs
organise your backpack   write your book review

36 Listen to Lucas and Nina talking about their school. What have they already done? What haven't they done yet? Copy the chart and put a tick (✔) or a cross (✗) next to the activities.

	Lucas	Nina
take the test		
hand in the research		
go to an art club meeting		
start the essay		

37 Listen again. Make sentences about 36. Follow the example.

1 take the test

   Lucas hasn't taken the test yet.

   Nina has already taken the test. She took it on Tuesday.

2 hand in the research

   ❓

3 go to an art club meeting

   ❓

4 start the essay

   ❓

I Can

- **talk about school activities and homework.**
- **say what I have and haven't done.**

unit 2

AMAZING YOUNG PEOPLE

23

1 Most of us dream of doing great things during our lifetime. Read and listen to these popular life dreams. Which ones do you hope to achieve?

Dreams

- Climb Mount Everest
- Meet a world leader
- Ride a camel or an elephant
- Learn how to play the piano, the guitar or the violin
- Be a contestant on a game or reality show
- Take award-winning photos of nature
- Help the poor and those in need
- Speak another language or two
- Travel around the world
- Become a doctor and work in a developing country
- Start a company
- Become a millionaire
- Write and publish a book

2 Do a class survey. Find out which of the dreams in **1** are the three favourites.

24

Listen. You will hear about some amazing young people and what they've achieved. As you listen, find answers to the questions.

1   **a** When was Yifan born?

b Where is she from?

c What has she achieved?

"I believe you should have goals and reach them step by step."
Hou Yifan

2   **a** When was William born?

b Where is he from?

c What has he achieved?

"With hard work, anything in life is possible."
William Kamkwamba

3 **a** When was Johnny born?

b Where is he from?

c What has he achieved?

"Pursue your dreams... Even if you don't succeed, if you try your hardest, the experience will help you..."
Johnny Strange

4   Work with a partner. Talk about the people in 3.

Who do you think is the most amazing young person?

Johnny Strange. He's been climbing mountains since he was twelve!

THINK BIG How do you set and achieve your goals? Which of the people in 3 do you agree with the most? Why?

Unit 2   21

Listen and read. Why is Jimmy different from the kids around him?

JIMMY WOODARD:
COMPUTER WHIZZ-KID
by Chris Winger

Where do you see yourself at seventeen? Owning a business? Owning a car? Saving for university? Chances are you will eventually do these things but maybe not when you are seventeen... unless you are someone like Jimmy Woodard!

Jimmy Woodard is a high school pupil from Manchester, Vermont, USA. In many ways, Jimmy is a normal teenager who spends a lot of time online every day. But in other ways, Jimmy has always been different from the kids around him. When Jimmy was very young, his parents realised he had a special gift. While other children were playing with toys, Jimmy would take his toys apart to find out how they worked. But Jimmy's gift really became obvious when he started using computers. Jimmy was only six when he started using his parents' computer. That's not so unusual these days. However, in Jimmy's case, if he had a problem with the computer, he worked out how to fix it by himself!

When Jimmy was in the 5th year of primary school, his technology teacher gave him a computer to work on. Jimmy took the computer apart and put it back together again. Since then, Jimmy has been working with computers in his school, even helping teachers with their technology problems.

When he was fourteen, Jimmy decided to open his own technology consulting company. Since that time, he has brought in about 200 regular customers. One of them is former astronaut Gerald Carr. "It feels funny sometimes," said Jimmy with a smile. "I can't believe I'm helping an astronaut with his computer!"

Jimmy has done more than just work on computers. Since he was eleven or twelve, Jimmy has been helping and working in his community. He has managed the sound and lights for a local TV show and for theatrical performances. Jimmy has also worked as a DJ. "I've been a DJ at more than fifty dance events already," he said. "It's really fun."

Jimmy has saved a lot of money over the past three years. "I've just bought my own car," he said happily. "I've used some of my money to buy more computers or equipment for my company. But I'm trying to save the rest of it for university." As for his future, Jimmy explained, "I don't know what I want to do yet. I know I want to do something with computers. But I'm interested in a lot of different things. I'd like to live in a big city someday. I can't wait to see what happens next."

READING COMPREHENSION

 **Number the events in the order they happened in Jimmy's life.**

a   Jimmy rebuilt a computer.

b   Jimmy bought a car.

c   Jimmy started his own company.

d   Jimmy took his toys apart to find out how they worked.

e   Jimmy started using his parents' computer.

 What do you think Jimmy will choose to do in the future? Why?

Language in Action

27

7 Listen and read. What has Zack been doing on the computer?

Mum: Zack, you've been on the computer for a while now.

Zack: I know. I've got to write a biography about an amazing person, so I've been doing research on someone. This guy is so interesting!

Mum: Who is it?

Zack: William Kamkwamba. He's been a builder and an inventor since he was a teenager.

Mum: What has he built?

Zack: His village in Malawi had no electricity or running water. So he built a windmill. And he was only fourteen!

Mum: Wow. How did he know how to make a windmill?

Zack: He got some books from the library and studied the diagrams.

Mum: He made a windmill from a diagram? That's amazing!

Zack: I know!

8 Practise the dialogue in 7 with a partner.

28

9 Listen and complete the sentences. Use the correct form of the verb.

> dance
> design computer programs
> do medical research
> play in rock bands

1 She's ___been dancing___ since __she was about five__ .

2 He's ? for ?.

3 He's ? for ?.

4 They've ? together since ?.

> How long **has** she **played** the piano?
> She**'s played** the piano <u>for</u> five years.
>
> How long **have** they **known** about William Kamkwamba?
> They**'ve known** about him <u>since</u> they saw a film about him.

10 Read the information and then complete the sentences about each amazing person. Use the present perfect and *for* or *since*.

> Hou Yifan is nineteen and a chess player. She started playing chess when she was three.

1 She ? chess ? sixteen years.

2 She ? chess ? she was three.

3 He ? mountains ? he was twelve.

4 He ? mountains ? ten years.

> Johnny Strange is twenty-two and a mountain climber. He started climbing when he was twelve.

> How long **has** your brother **been playing** tennis?
> He**'s been playing** tennis <u>since</u> he was five.
>
> How long **have** you and your sister **been bungee jumping**?
> We**'ve been bungee jumping** <u>for</u> two years.

11 Read the answers. Ask the questions. Use the present perfect continuous.

1 ?

He's been saving money for university since he was thirteen.

2 ?

We've been volunteering at the hospital for two years.

3 ?

She's been filming her documentary since August.

4 ?

I've been playing the piano since I was at nursery school.

5 ?

They've been friends for seven years.

12 What's a 'gifted child'? Choose one answer. Do you know any gifted children in history?

a a young person who's good at exams and tests

b a young person with an exceptional talent, skill or ability

c a young person with a rich family and lots of possessions

30

13 Listen and read. Then answer the questions.

1 Who went to Harvard?   **2** Who was from Brazil?   **3** Who was blind?

> **CONTENT WORDS**
> ability   co-found   compose   determined   exceptional talent
> gifted   inspiration   keep in touch   legend   social media   symphony

Amazing Young People Through the Ages

1 Do you think children are too young to make a difference in the world? Do you think only adults can start companies or win awards? If so, think again! Throughout history, there have always been gifted young people with exceptional talents and abilities for their age. As children or teenagers, they did amazing things that changed lives. Read on for inspiration!

2 Wolfgang Amadeus Mozart was one very famous gifted child. He could play the piano at the age of three and the violin at six. Amadeus composed his first symphony at the age of eight and wrote an opera at fourteen. He went on to become one of the most important composers of all time.

A	B	C	D	E	F	G	H	I	J
K	L	M	N	O	P	Q	R	S	T
U	V	W	X	Y	Z				
# 1	2	3	4	5	6	7	8	9 0	# 2001

3 Louis Braille was born in France in 1809. He started working on a special alphabet (later called Braille) to help blind people to read, when he was just twelve years old. Louis lost his eyesight in an accident at the age of three but he was determined to create a system to help blind people. Today, blind people all over the world communicate using Braille.

4 Fourteen-year-old Nadia Comaneci scored a perfect ten in gymnastics at the 1976 Olympic Games. She was the first person ever to do this! People still remember Nadia for her exceptional skills and abilities as a gymnast.

5 Pelé was only seventeen when he scored six goals in four games in the 1958 World Cup, making Brazil the football champions that year. He later became a football legend and a national hero. He was listed in the Guinness Book of Records as the professional footballer with the highest number of goals in his career.

6 What about young people and technology? Mark Zuckerberg was only nineteen when he started Facebook with some friends of his at Harvard University. Although it hardly needs an introduction, Facebook is a social media platform that has changed the way people around the world keep in touch with each other. Also at nineteen, Steve Jobs was learning the skills that helped him create Apple and Bill Gates was getting ready to co-found a company called Microsoft!

14 **Look at 13. Copy the chart in your notebook and complete.**

Who?	What?	Age?
1 ?	began to work on a special alphabet for blind readers	2 ?
3 ?	helped his national team win the World Cup	4 ?
5 ?	scored a perfect 10 at the Olympics	6 ?
Wolfgang Amadeus Mozart	7 ?	8
Mark Zuckerberg	8 ?	19

15 **Look at 13. Correct the sentences.**

1 Louis Braille was born blind.

2 Braille isn't very popular now.

3 No one knows who Nadia Comaneci is these days.

4 Pele is in the Guinness Book of Records because of his 1958 World Cup performance.

5 Mark Zuckerberg created Facebook alone.

16 **Work in groups. Read and answer the questions.**

1 Which person or people in the article do you admire the most? Explain why.

2 Look at the pairs of special and gifted people in this unit. Can you say what they have in common?

Johnny Strange and Pelé

William Kamkwamba and Jimmy Woodard

Mark Zuckerberg and Bill Gates

Nadia Comaneci and Pelé

17 **Choose a person in 16. Write an entry for a Gifted Child fact file in your notebook. Use these headings and add your ideas.**

Fact file
Name:
Born: (when? where?)
Why he/she is special:
Extra information:
Information sources:

18 Listen and read. Where did Daniel go last summer? What has his dad learnt to make?

32

Daniel:	We went to Japan last summer. Have you ever been there?
Grace:	No, I haven't. What was it like?
Daniel:	Amazing. We stayed for two weeks and I didn't want to leave! I want to go back next year. I've even started learning Japanese.
Grace:	Wow. Did you like the food there?
Daniel:	Yes, I loved it. My favourite dish was sashimi. Have you ever tried it?
Grace:	No, I haven't. I've never eaten Japanese food.
Daniel:	Well, basically it's raw fish.
Grace:	Raw fish? That sounds weird.
Daniel:	It's delicious! And my dad has learnt to make it. He made octopus sashimi for us last Saturday. And he's making eel sashimi for dinner this Saturday! Would you like to come?
Grace:	Er... thanks but um... I think I'm busy on Saturday.

19 Look at 18 and complete.

The Past Simple Tense	We use the past simple tense for events at a particular time (**on**, **at**, **in**, **last**, **ago**, **when**, ...). We **went** to Japan ¹ 🔧 . ² 🔧 the food there? (when you were on holiday) My dad ³ 🔧 octopus sashimi ⁴ 🔧 .
The Present Perfect Tense	We use the present perfect tense for special events in our lives (**ever**, **never**): I **have seen** the Leaning Tower of Pisa. **Have** you **ever** been to Japan? ⁵ 🔧 sashimi? I ⁶ 🔧 Japanese food.
	We also use the present perfect tense for facts in a period up to now (**for**, **since**): We **have lived** in Istanbul **for** four years. (We live there now.) My dad **has worked** at this factory **since** September.

 Read and choose the correct form of the verbs in brackets.

1   I live in Cairo. (I lived/I have lived) here for ten years.

2   Last Saturday, (we visited/we have visited) my grandparents.

3   **A:** My brother's only ten but he can drive a car.

   B: Really? When (did he learn/has he learnt)?

4   (Did you fall/Have you fallen) off your bike on Saturday?

5   (I knew/I have known) my best friend since we were three. I love her!

6   Where (did you buy/have you bought) that amazing hat?

 Complete the paragraph with the correct form of the verbs in brackets.

My grandfather is an amazing man. He's a photographer and he has always loved travelling. He ¹ (travel) all over the world in his life and he still goes abroad every year. He ² (fly) to China when he was sixty years old and ³ (stay) with a family there. He ⁴ (take) lots of wonderful pictures of the Great Wall while he was there. He ⁵ (also go) to Africa quite a few times in his life. Two years ago, he ⁶ (go) to Kenya. He ⁷ (go) on a balloon trip there and ⁸ (take) some beautiful photos of wild animals from the air. I ⁹ (never, leave) the UK so I am a bit jealous of him! What about you? ¹⁰ (you, ever, visit) any interesting countries?

Work with a partner. Choose a topic, then ask and answer. Then change partners and talk again.

1 Abroad
Have you ever been abroad? Where did you go? When did you go there? Who did you go with? How long did you stay there?

2 Cinema
How many good films have you seen this year? What was the best one called? When did you see it? Where did you see it? Who did you see it with?

3 Food
Have you ever eaten anything weird? What was it? Where did you eat it? When did you eat it? Who made it? Did you enjoy it?

4 Places
Have you ever visited a really interesting place? What was this place? When did you visit it? Who took you there? How did you get there? How long did you stay there? Did you take pictures there?

Seeds of Peace

1   Throughout history, there has hardly ever been a moment when the whole world was at peace. There have been world wars between many countries, and also countless conflicts between two nations. Unfortunately, there still are. Every day, we hear about individuals, politicians and world leaders trying to bring peace to countries at war. They sometimes succeed, but often they don't. However, there's another group of people you probably haven't heard about who are trying to do the same thing. Their message is more hopeful because they're young. They're mainly teenagers who have seen war and conflict and want to change things. These teenagers belong to an organisation called Seeds of Peace.

2   Seeds of Peace was started in 1993 by a journalist named John Wallach. The group began with just 46 teenagers and educators. Since then, it has grown to over 5,000 participants from 27 different countries.

 23   **Look at the questions. Answer with a partner, then share your ideas with the class.**

1   Which countries in the world are at war today? Do you know why there's conflict?

2   Have there been big wars in your country in the past? When were they?

3   What's the best way to stop a war, in your opinion?

    a   with an army and soldiers

    b   with political leaders and discussions

    c   by changing how people in the countries feel

 24   **Read the article quickly. Match the main ideas a–f to paragraphs 1–5.**

a   Seeds of Peace was started more than twenty years ago.

b   When they go home, the young people have got more hope about living in peace one day.

c   At a Seeds of Peace camp, people talk about their problems and learn to live together.

d   Politicians and world leaders can't always solve problems.

e   The organisation brings together young people in summer camps.

f   There's always been conflict in the world and it's difficult to resolve.

3 Each summer, 350 new 'Seeds' from countries in conflict are carefully chosen by the Seeds of Peace organisation. This group of teenagers attends the Seeds of Peace international summer camp, where they meet and live with other teenagers whose countries are 'enemy' countries. The camp provides a neutral environment where young people can discuss the issues between their countries and talk about their personal experiences. As they do this, the campers learn important communication skills as well as conflict resolution and critical thinking skills. Before the camp is over, they've opened themselves up to new perspectives. Most importantly, they've learnt how to make change happen.

4 Fifteen-year-old Sharon Koren from Israel summed up her expectations of the summer camp with these words: "My goal is to be as understanding as I can be, to be open to hear the other side and respect everyone. Everyone wants peace... I think we're going to make peace."

5 After the summer camp is over, these teenagers return to their countries. They go home, not just with memories of new friendships but also with the idea that they can be leaders who can work together for a better future for themselves and for the whole world. They've learnt that the fighting around them doesn't have to go on forever.

33

25 **Listen and read. Choose the correct words.**

1 Seeds of Peace was started by (a group of educators/a journalist).

2 The teenagers who become Seeds (have never seen/have experienced) conflict in their countries.

3 At the camp, young people (work in groups to create/talk to people from) 'enemy' countries.

4 The camp helps young people to (talk about conflict/learn about conflict in their country).

26 **Look at the names of three more youth organisations. Quickly research each organisation and match it to an aim. Which organisation do you think is the most useful?**

1 International Youth Climate Movement

2 Hip Hop 4 Life (US)

3 Erasmus Student Exchange Program

a environmental inspiration

b experience other cultures

c health and essential life skills

THINK BIG Why do you think Seeds of Peace campers are more hopeful about world peace after the camp? Are there summer camps in your country? What do people learn there?

27 Read the biography.

My Brother Josh

My brother Josh is amazing! He was born in 1998 in Melbourne, Australia. Josh went to Melmoth Primary School there and was top of his class.

In 2008, my family moved to Bristol, in the UK. Josh has been very busy since we moved. He has played the drums with the school band, has been on the school football team and has joined the drama club.

Josh is really busy but he always takes time out to do things with me. That's what makes him so amazing!

28 Look at 27. Copy and complete the timeline about Josh.

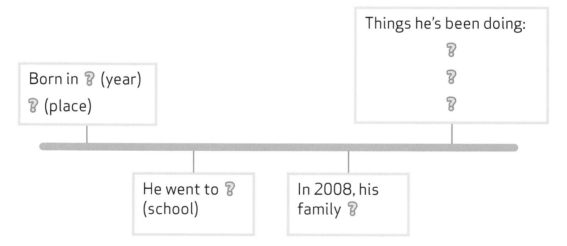

Things he's been doing:
?
?
?

Born in ? (year)
? (place)

He went to ? (school)

In 2008, his family ?

29 Write a short biography.

1 Interview an older relative or do research on an amazing person that you're interested in.

2 Create a timeline based on your interview or research.

3 Use your timeline to write the biography.

4 Share your biography with a partner. Discuss each other's work.

30 Just like the young people in this unit, all of us have amazing qualities and talents. Copy and complete a chart about you.

1 Think about your good qualities and talents.

2 Complete the first and second columns of the chart.

3 Ask a partner to name three things about you that are amazing.

4 Write them in the third column of the chart.

	My good qualities	What I'm good at	My classmate thinks I'm amazing because . . .
Ex.	I'm friendly.	playing the drums	I'm quite clever.
1.	?	?	?
2.	?	?	?
3.	?	?	?

31 Now study your chart. Is your classmate's opinion of you the same as/different to your opinion about yourself?

PROJECT

32 Make an Amazing Me collage.

1 Include photos or drawings of yourself doing things you enjoy.

2 Include drawings, pictures from magazines and words and phrases that show who you are and what you like.

3 Write your name on the back and display your collage in the classroom.

33 Take turns guessing the person who made each collage. Then interview that person.

THINK BIG How can we make use of other people's opinions of us? Whose opinion counts the most?

Listening and Speaking

 34 Listen, read and repeat.

1 spl **2** squ **3** thr

 35 Listen and blend the sounds.

1	spl-a-sh	splash	**2**	squ-i-d	squid
3	thr-ee	three	**4**	spl-i-t	split
5	squ-a-sh	squash	**6**	thr -oa-t	throat

 36 Listen and chant.

> Take a dive in the deep blue sea.
> Splish! Splash!
> One squid, two whales
> And three dolphins, swimming free.

37 Work in a small group. Play a memory game. Follow the steps below.

know   live   play   study   watch

1 Take turns making sentences with the verbs from the box. Follow the order shown. Here's an example:

Mary (Pupil 1): I've known Ben since I was six years old.

Tom (Pupil 2): Mary has known Ben since she was six years old. I've lived in Liverpool for ten years.

Anna (Pupil 3): Mary has known Ben since she was six years old. Tom has lived in Liverpool for ten years. I've been playing football since I was in Year 1.

2 Continue with the other verbs until a pupil can't remember all the sentences. Then start again with *know*.

Ed (Pupil 4): Mary has known Ben since... oh, no! I forget! Let's start again.

3 Talk about how you did as a group. Which pupil remembered the most sentences?

38 Read and complete. Use the correct form of the words in the box.

> be   discuss   not do   live   meet

This is Jen and Leyla. Jen ¹ **?** in Oxford since 2008. Leyla has been Jen's best friend for two years. They ² **?** each other when they ³ **?** in Year 3. They like in-line skating but Jen ⁴ **?** it since she was a little girl. Leyla's teaching her how to do it again. A few weeks ago they ⁵ **?** about inviting their friends to skate with them at the park. Maybe they'll go next weekend.

39 Complete the sentences. Use the present perfect continuous and for or since.

> have cooking lessons   play football
> practise the piano   sing opera

1 She **?** she was six years old.

2 She **?** the past eight years.

3 They **?** Year 4.

4 He **?** an hour.

I Can

- talk about past experiences.

- talk about amazing people's accomplishments (including my own).

unit 3 DILEMMAS

38

1 Listen and read. What would you do? Work with a group to choose an answer for each situation. Then compare and discuss answers with another group.

Your older sister is supposed to be home by 10:00 p.m. One night, you see your sister leave at 9:00. At 10:00, your sister still isn't home. You're worried about her but if you tell your parents, your sister will get into trouble. And she might be just a few minutes late. But something might be wrong!

Answer 1: You should tell your parents right away.
Answer 2: You should wait an hour before you tell them. Everything is probably OK.

Two classmates have found the answer key to a Maths test near the photocopier. You see them pick it up and hear them talking about it. They tell you that they'll show you the answers if you don't tell anyone. You're not doing well in Maths. You really need to pass this test. If you look at the answers and cheat in the test, you'll feel guilty and dishonest but you'll pass. If you tell the teacher about the answer key, the boys will be angry and you probably won't pass.

Answer 1: You should talk to the boys and tell them to put the answer key back or you'll tell the teacher.
Answer 2: You should look at the answer key and not tell the teacher.
Answer 3: You should just tell the boys you're not interested and walk away.

2 You'll hear three people talking about dilemmas or difficult situations they've experienced. Listen. Then read about their concerns.

Dilemma #1

If I keep the wallet, I'll feel guilty.

Emily

Dilemma #2

If I tell my friend I lost her necklace, she'll be upset with me.

Angela

Dilemma #3

If I confess I broke the lamp, I'll get into trouble.

Al

 3 What's the right thing to do? Think of advice to give to Emily, Angela and Al. Then listen and compare your answers.

1 Emily, I think you should ⁇ .

2 Angela, I think you should ⁇ .

3 Al, I think you should ⁇ .

 4 Work with a partner. Talk about the dilemmas.
Use the expressions in the box or your own ideas.

be upset with (him/her)
feel good
feel guilty
get into trouble

What will happen if Emily returns the wallet?

If she returns the wallet, she'll feel good! And the man will, too!

 THINK BIG How do you cope with dilemmas? Who do you discuss them with? Why?

5 Listen and read. What's Marissa's dilemma?

MARISSA MOBLEY'S
DILEMMA

by Milan Norman

Marissa Mobley walked into the kitchen and said, "I'm home." She didn't sound happy. Mrs Mobley looked at Marissa.

"Is something wrong?" she asked. "You don't sound happy."

"Oh, nothing, Mum," Marissa replied. "I've just got a lot of homework."

Mrs Mobley looked worried. "Are you sure you're OK?" she asked again.

"Umm… yeah, Mum. I've just been doing too much at school lately. So I'm tired. That's all," Marissa said as she walked into her room and closed the door.

Marissa's brother, Leo, knocked on Marissa's door. "Hey, what's up?" asked Leo. "Something's wrong. I can see it in your face."

"Well," said Marissa, finally, "can you keep a secret? I've got a problem at school. It's a real dilemma. You know Dan, right?"

"Dan? Yeah, I know him," said Leo. "He's a funny guy."

"Well, I don't think he's so funny. At least not this week," Marissa said. "Listen to this. He asked me to help him cheat in our Maths test on Friday."

"What?" Leo asked.

"I guess Dan's marks in Maths aren't very good this term," said Marissa. "If he doesn't do well in the test, he won't be able to play for the basketball team any more. He sits next to me in Maths and he knows I do well in tests. He wants me to make it easy for him to see my paper during the test."

"Seriously?" said Leo. "That's not good."

"I know," said Marissa, sounding more and more upset. "I've been thinking about it all week and it's bothering me a lot. I'd like to help Dan but helping him cheat really isn't helping him! I just can't do it!"

"Of course you can't!" her brother said. "If a boy asks you to help him cheat in a test, you should tell your teacher!"

"Tell my teacher? If I do that, Dan will get into *big* trouble," said Marissa.

"But if you help him cheat, you'll be cheating, too, Marissa," said Leo.

Marissa sighed. After a minute, she smiled and looked at her brother. "I know!" she said.

"What are you going to do?" Leo asked.

"Wait and see," Marissa answered. Then she picked up her mobile phone.

READING COMPREHENSION

6 **Find one detail in the story that supports these statements.**

1 Marissa's mum knows Marissa isn't happy.

2 Marissa doesn't tell her mum the truth about her problem.

3 Marissa trusts her brother Leo.

4 Leo doesn't want Marissa to help Dan cheat.

5 Marissa doesn't think telling the teacher is a good idea.

6 Marissa's got an idea about what to do.

THINK BIG Why do you think Marissa has been having a hard time deciding what to do? What do you think she's going to do next? Why?

7 Listen and read. What should Chris do?

Ashley: This is fun! Can we play *Lost World 3* next?

Chris: Uh, no. We can't. The disc is broken.

Ashley: Broken? How'd that happen?

Chris: I was running to catch the bus and I dropped it. Before I could pick it up, someone stepped on it.

Ashley: Oh, no. Did you tell Sam? He's going to be upset.

Chris: No, I haven't told him yet. I was hoping he would forget that I borrowed it from him.

Ashley: But you've got to tell him! He won't be upset if you replace it. You can buy him a new disc with your pocket money.

Chris: You're right. I'll buy him a new one and tell him what happened.

8 Practise the dialogue in 7 with a partner.

9 Listen and complete the sentences.

1 If she tells the truth, ? .

2 If she keeps it, ? .

3 If he goes to the concert, ? .

4 If he doesn't tell his mum what's wrong, ? .

> **If** he **pays attention** in class, he**'ll understand** the lesson.
>
> **If** they **don't study** for the Maths test, they **won't get** a good mark.
>
> **If** you **tell** me the truth, I**'ll help** you.
>
> **Tip:** Use a conditional sentence to express true or factual ideas in the present or future.

10 **Complete the sentences. What will they do?**

1   If my older brother wants me to lie for him, (I/not do) ❓ it.

2   If Sarah says bad things about Michelle, (I/change) ❓ the subject.

3   If you help me with my book review, (I/help) ❓ you with your project.

4   If you tell Mum we lent Anna her CD, (she/be) ❓ upset.

5   (I/not read) ❓ my sister's diary if I see it on her desk.

> You **should tell** your parents **if** you've got a problem at school.
>
> **If** you don't want to get into trouble, you **shouldn't lie**.

11 **Which is the best advice? Make sentences with** should **or** shouldn't.

1   You see someone being bullied.

   a   Just walk away.   **ⓑ** Tell an adult.

2   You tear an expensive shirt in the changing room in a shop.

   a   Quietly return it to the rack.   **b**   Tell a shop assistant what happened.

3   Your brother's going to watch a film that he's not allowed to see.

   a   Tell your parents about it.   **b**   Don't say anything to your parents.

4   Your sister's studying and you want to listen to music.

   a   Tell her to go to a friend's house.   **b**   Use headphones.

5   Your friend asks you to let him copy your English homework.

   a   Tell your teacher.   **b**   Offer to help him do his homework.

12 Look at the questions. Answer with a partner, then share your ideas with the class.

1 Think of something you did in the past that you knew was wrong.

2 How did you feel?

3 Did you do anything about it? Why/Why not?

46

13 Listen and read. What's ethical behaviour? Choose one answer.

a Doing the fair and acceptable thing in a situation.

b Always being kind to people.

c Doing what you want to do in a situation.

CONTENT WORDS

acceptable   according to   based on   ethical   ethics   excuse
harmless   morally   perspective   respectful   traits   treat

---

Ethics

1   The saying 'Treat others the way you'd want them to treat you' isn't hard to understand. It means that you should behave towards others the way you'd want them to behave towards you. It sounds simple but isn't always simple to do. If everyone followed this advice, the world would be a much better place.

2   This unit is about ethics and ethical behaviour. Do you know what 'ethics' are? Of course you do. You make choices based on ethics all the time. Ethics tell you what's right or wrong, fair or unfair, acceptable or unacceptable in a situation. Choosing to do the right thing is ethical behaviour.

3   The word *ethics* comes from the Greek word *ethos*, which means 'character'. Our character is all of our traits and qualities taken together. It helps us decide what's right or wrong. What kind of 'character' have you got? Are you respectful of your classmates? Would you cheat in a test to make sure you pass? Would you tell a 'harmless' lie in order to avoid hurting someone's feelings? Would you lie to someone to get out of trouble? These are all questions of ethics.

4   How can you choose ethical behaviour in a difficult situation? You can begin by asking yourself a few questions but your answers must be honest. The first question is, "If I do it, will I feel bad afterwards?" If we do something that's morally wrong, we'll feel guilty about it, even if we can find excuses for our actions. The second question is, "If I do it, will it hurt somebody?" If the answer is yes, then it might not be the right thing to do. You can also ask, "How would I judge someone else who did the same thing? What would my mum or dad say about it?" This helps us see things from the right perspective. And a final but very important question is, "What's my gut feeling about it?" This can give you a good idea of whether your behaviour is ethical or not.

5   Behaving according to your ethics isn't the easiest thing to do but it's definitely always the right thing to do.

14 Look at 13. Read and say true or false.

1 The first paragraph says that if someone hurts you, you should hurt them.

2 We use ethics in our everyday lives.

3 If you want to make an ethical decision, you need to be honest with yourself.

4 If we can find a good excuse for our actions, we won't feel guilty.

5 It's helpful to think about what our parents would say.

6 Following our ethics is sometimes difficult but we should always try to do it.

15 Work with a partner. Read the stories and decide who made a good ethical decision. Share your opinions with the class.

1 George went into a changing room to try on a pair of jeans. On the floor, he found five one hundred-euro notes. He put the money in his pocket. He paid for the jeans with some of the money. Later, he gave the rest to charity.

2 Jennifer visited a friend for the weekend. While she was in the living room, she accidentally knocked over a valuable vase. She quickly collected the pieces and threw them away without telling anyone about it.

3 Paul's teacher asked Paul and Dan to do a Maths project together. Paul doesn't like Dan. Paul is good at Maths and he can do the project without Dan. Paul worked with Dan and helped him answer the questions.

16 Answer Hande's email. Write in your notebook. Give her the best advice you can.

TO	agonyaunt@iMail.com
CC	
SUBJECT	Please help?

Hi,

I'm very confused and I don't know what to do. I'd really like your advice.

Last week, I heard a big secret about a girl in my class. Her name's Fiona. Fiona doesn't like me. Yesterday, Fiona told some lies about me and now my best friend isn't talking to me! If I tell everyone Fiona's secret, they won't listen to her any more, but it'll hurt Fiona. What should I do?

Love,
Hande

Grammar

17 Listen and read. Why does Ryan want to walk across the field? Why doesn't Holly want to walk across it?

Ryan:	If we walk across this field, we'll get to my house faster.
Holly:	But the farmer might get angry if we walk across his field.
Ryan:	No, he won't. My dad's the farmer and this is his field!
Holly:	Oh.
Ryan:	Come on. If we hurry, we may be in time for the cartoon show.
Holly:	I don't want to go across that field. Those bulls could chase us if we go near them.
Ryan:	Holly, they aren't bulls.
Holly:	And I'm wearing a red jumper. You shouldn't go near bulls if you're wearing red clothes.
Ryan:	They're cows, not bulls. Even if we walk really close to them, they'll just carry on eating.
Holly:	What should we do if they charge us?
Ryan:	Listen, if they charge us, we'll climb that big tree.
Holly:	OK, but I'll only do it if we swap jumpers first.

18 Look at 17 and complete.

if clause	result clause
If we **walk** across this field,	we ¹ 👤 to my house faster.
If we **walk** across this field,	the farmer ² 👤 angry.
If we **hurry**,	we ³ 👤 in time for the cartoon show.
If we **go** near those bulls,	they ⁴ 👤 us.
If you**'ve got** red clothes on,	you ⁵ 👤 near bulls.
If they **charge** us,	we ⁶ 👤 that big tree.

Tip: Use **may (not)**, **might (not)**, and **could** when you aren't sure what will happen. Use **should (not)** to give advice.

19  Read and match.

1	If we don't take a map,	**a**	I may go to the beach.
2	If you come to my house,	**b**	we could make pancakes together.
3	If it's nice weather tomorrow,	**c**	we might get lost.

20 Read and complete using the correct form of the verbs. Then choose the correct words to complete the sentences.

1   If we ___don't hurry___ (not hurry), we (might/*might not*) catch the bus.

2   If football practice ❓ (finish) late tonight, you (should/shouldn't) tell your mum.

3   Kemal (should/shouldn't) eat so much sugar if he ❓ (want) to have good teeth.

4   Martha (might/might not) get into the team if she ❓ (practise) a lot.

5   If I ❓ (enter) this competition, I (could/could not) win a camera.

6   If you ❓ (not put) your keys in a safe place, you (may/should) lose them.

21 Read and complete. Use the phrases in the box.

> bring some sandwiches   could get really hungry   is sunny   may come
> might get quite cold   says it's OK   should we do   want to go to the lake

Zoe: Let's go for a bike ride tomorrow if it ¹❓ again.

Ben: OK. But what ²❓ if the weather isn't good?

Zoe: It'll be good. Look at that amazing sunset.

Ben: You never know. If the wind gets worse, it ³❓.

Zoe: I don't think it will. Let's plan our day out.

Ben: Well, if we ⁴❓, we should get up early. It's quite a long way.

Zoe: Yes. And if we're out all day, we ⁵❓.

Ben: That's true. So if I ⁶❓, will you bring some water?

Zoe: OK. And Leyla says she ⁷❓ if her dad ⁸❓.

Ben: Great!

22 Make sentences for these situations. Collect ideas with your class, then write in your notebook.

What might you do...

• if it's hot tomorrow?

• if you've got enough money this weekend?

• if you've got time tomorrow?

• if your parents let you?

What should you do...

• if you cut your finger?

• if you can't sleep at night?

• if you find a mobile phone in the street?

• if you don't understand your homework?

Proverbs from Around the World

1   Every culture has got its own proverbs. Proverbs are short sayings about life that are passed on from generation to generation. They go back tens, hundreds or even thousands of years and sum up the practical experience of the people who use them. Because proverbs give sound advice, they help us make decisions. The Chinese proverb, ¹ ❓ is a good example. Anyone who's about to make a hasty decision, without weighing up the pros and cons first, is warned of the horrible consequences of a bad choice.

2   Sometimes proverbs can seem to have different meanings. The English proverb, ² ❓ is one example. Some think that the proverb is a warning for people who keep moving and never settle down. If these people 'gather no moss', then it means they've achieved nothing. Others think that the proverb is a warning for people who never do

23   Look at two famous sayings in English. What do you think they mean? Share your ideas with the class. Are there similar sayings in your culture?

    1   Never judge a book by its cover.   2   A friend's eye is a good mirror.

24   Read the article quickly and match the sayings to places 1–5.

  a   A rolling stone gathers no moss.

  b   Don't think there are no crocodiles just because the water is calm.

  c   Little by little, the camel goes into the couscous.

  d   You'll reap what you sow.

  e   One step in the wrong direction can cause a thousand years of regret.

anything. If you don't move and change with the times, you'll become like an old mossy piece of rock.

3   We often find that there are similar proverbs across cultures. Maybe this is because proverbs have travelled and have been translated from one language to another or maybe it's because they're just common sense. A similar expression to ³❓ appears in many languages and it simply means that you'll get what you give. Other proverbs use colourful images from the culture of the people who

tell them, like the Moroccan proverb, ⁴❓, which means that you can't force things – everything happens in its own time. Being relaxed about time is an important part of Moroccan culture. One proverb in Malaysia, where crocodiles are common, is ⁵❓.

4   Whatever advice they give, one thing all proverbs teach us is that although societies are changing and becoming more advanced every day, there are some basic facts about life and human nature that will never change.

49

25 Listen and read. Check your answers in 24.

26 Look at 24. Correct the sentences. Use the words in the article.

1 Proverbs are stories and legends about life in different cultures.

2 Proverbs don't give us good advice.

3 Proverbs are always easy to understand.

4 Proverbs are different in every country and culture.

5 Moroccan people like working fast and being on time.

6 Life and human nature is always changing and advancing.

27 Work in groups. Think of three proverbs in your culture and explain their meaning in English. Which proverb do you think is the most useful?

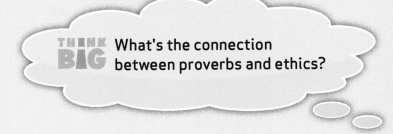

THINK BIG What's the connection between proverbs and ethics?

28 Work with a partner. Answer questions about 'Marissa Mobley's Dilemma' (see pages 38–39).

1 Who are the characters in 'Marissa Mobley's Dilemma'?

2 How does Marissa feel when she gets home from school?

3 Who knocks on Marissa's door?

4 What's Marissa's dilemma?

5 What advice does Marissa's brother give her?

6 At the end of the story on page 39, what do you think Marissa is going to do?

29 How do you think the story ends? Discuss these possible endings with a partner. Think of a reason why each one is possible.

• Marissa helps Dan cheat.

Reason: 🔑

• Marissa tells her teacher about Dan.

Reason: 🔑

• Marissa tells Dan she can't help him.

Reason: 🔑

• Marissa helps Dan study.

Reason: 🔑

30 With your partner, write an ending to the story. Add details, such as how the other story characters react to Marissa's decision and how she feels about it.

31 Share your story ending with another pair. Discuss. Talk about what Marissa did and whether it was the right thing to do.

THINK BIG Do you always know what the right thing to do is? How do you know what's right? Why isn't it always easy to do the right thing?

32 Read about three situations and three possible courses of action for each one. Which one is the right thing to do? Discuss with a partner.

Situation	#1	#2	#3
You're getting into your mum's car. You see an envelope full of money on the ground.	Tell your mum about it and ask if you can keep the money.	Pick up the money quietly but don't tell your mum about it.	Tell your mum and ask her how you can return the money.
Your teacher gives you the highest mark for your book review and uses it as a model for the rest of the class. Your older sister wrote the book review for you.	Do nothing. Be happy and accept the mark and the compliment.	Tell your teacher you didn't write the review and apologise.	Tell your parents what you did but don't tell your teacher.
Your teacher goes out of the room during a big test. Your classmate, who's the best pupil in the class, tries to show you her answers.	Copy your classmate's answers – after all, she offered. It'd be silly to say no.	Compare your answers with hers but change only a few to match hers.	Tell your classmate, "No, thank you".

PROJECT

33 Make a page to go in a class handbook about doing the right thing.

1 Choose a dilemma from the unit or use one of your own. Describe it at the top of the page.

2 Write three possible courses of action.

3 Use a picture from a magazine or draw one to show the right thing to do.

4 Present your page to the class. Read it aloud. Then say what you think the right thing to do is.

5 Bind the pages together to make a class handbook.

I think she should run after the man and return the tablet to him. If she doesn't, she'll feel terrible later.

Dilemma: You're at a park. You see a man sitting on a bench with a tablet. He leaves the park and you notice he's left his tablet on the bench. You've always wanted one but you haven't got enough money to buy one. What should you do?

1: Sit on the bench and cover the tablet so no one sees it.

2: Don't say anything but hold onto the tablet in case the man comes back for it. Secretly hope he doesn't!

3: Run after the man and return the tablet to him.

51

34 Listen, read and repeat.

1 nch   **2** nth   **3** mpt

 52

35 Listen and blend the sounds.

1 l-u-nch   lunch   **2** t-e-nth   tenth

3 p-r-o-mpt   prompt   **4** c-r-u-nch   crunch

5 m-o-nth   month   **6** t-e-mpt   tempt

 53

36 Listen and chant.

> I make lunch
> On the tenth of the month.
> An apple and crisps.
> Do you want any sweets?
> Don't tempt me!
> Crunch! Crunch!

Packed lunch

37 Work in groups of three. Choose a situation from the box or create your own. Pupils 1 and 2 role play the situation. Pupil 3 states the right thing to do.

Oh, no! My ball's just broken the window of that house!

If you break something, you should tell the owner.

You should go up to the front door and talk to the owner.

You:
- lose your friend's CD.
- see someone cheat in a test.
- spill juice on your friend's new shirt.
- see a man drop his wallet.
- break your friend's mobile phone.
- are asked to lie for your brother/sister.
- break a window at home.
- forget mother's day.

38 Complete the sentences with expressions from the box.

> be upset with   feel good about
> feel guilty (3x)   get into trouble

1 Claudia saw a man drop his wallet. When she picked it up, she saw that there was a lot of money in it. She was tempted to keep it but she knew it wasn't right. She thought about what to do. By the time she decided to return the man's wallet, he was gone. Claudia ❓. She ❓ herself for not deciding quickly enough.

2 Anna saw two classmates looking at each other's papers during an exam. She didn't know what to do. She knew it was wrong to cheat but she didn't want her friends to ❓. Anna ❓ about not saying anything.

3 Mike was at a toy shop and was holding a robot when he accidentally broke it. He didn't have the money to pay for the toy so he put it back on the shelf and quickly left the shop. Michael ❓. He didn't ❓ what he did.

39 Read the problems in 38 again. Choose one. In your notebook, write what you think the person should have done.

40 Look at the example. Read and complete. Use may, could and might not.

1 If I __'m__ (be) unkind to my friend, he ___may___ be sad.

2 If my classmate ❓ (not study), he ❓ get a low grade.

3 If she ❓ (spend) all her money, she ❓ have enough for the concert.

4 They ❓ get upset if we ❓ (break) their toys.

5 My mum ❓ feel sad if I ❓ (not tidy) my room.

6 If you ❓ (not eat) breakfast, you ❓ feel well by noon.

I Can

- **talk about consequences and possibilities and give advice.**
- **talk about doing the right thing.**

How Well Do I Know It? Can I Use It?

1 Think about it. Read and draw. Practise.

☺ I know this.   •• I need more practice.   ☹ I don't know this.

	PAGES	☺	••	☹
School Activities: study for a test, hand in an essay, finish a project...	5	☺	••	☹
Advice: be more careful, do it again...	5	☺	••	☹
Achievements: climb a mountain, start a company...	20-21	☺	••	☹
Dilemmas: (tell/don't tell) the truth, (return/don't return) a wallet, (cheat/don't cheat) in a test...	36-37	☺	••	☹
Results and Consequences: feel good, feel guilty, get into trouble...	37	☺	••	••
Has he **practised** his part <u>yet</u>? Yes, he **has**. He**'s** <u>already</u> **practised** his part. No, he **hasn't**. He **hasn't practised** it <u>yet</u>. **Have** the twins <u>ever</u> **studied** abroad? Yes, they **have**. / No, they **haven't**. My computer **has crashed** three times today.	8-9, 12-13	☺	••	☹
How long **has** he **played** the guitar? He**'s played** the guitar <u>for</u> five years. How long **has** she **been playing** in a band? She**'s been playing** in a band <u>since</u> she was fourteen.	24-25	☺	••	☹
We **have lived** here <u>for</u> three years. We **moved** here <u>in</u> 2012.	28-29	☺	••	☹
If he **studies** hard for the Maths test, he**'ll get** a good mark. You **should talk** to your parent if you **have** a problem.	40-41	☺	••	☹
If you **do** that, Dad **might/may** get angry. We **could/may** get lost **if** we **don't take** a map. **If** you **don't understand**, you **should** ask your teacher.	44-45	☺	••	☹

54

2 **Get ready.**

A Choose the correct word or phrase to complete the dialogue. Then listen and check.

Mum:	The school play is tomorrow night. Have you (learnt / learning) your lines yet?
Danny:	I've (learn / learnt) most of them already. We've been (practised / practising) for two weeks.
Mum:	Really? I didn't (know / known) that. Where have you (practise / been practising)?
Danny:	We've (practising / been practising) every day at school, after lunch. Yesterday we (practised / have practised) for a whole hour!
Mum:	And have you (studied / studying) for your Maths test tomorrow?
Danny:	Yeah, I (studied / 've studied) a bit last night.
Mum:	You should (study / studying) again after dinner tonight.
Danny:	But Mum, I need to (practise / practising) my lines for the play! If I (forget / forgot) my lines on stage, I'll (feel / feeling) awful.
Mum:	I know, Danny, but if you don't (pass / passing) your Maths test, you (might / should) feel even more awful and then you won't enjoy your play! Listen – study Maths for an hour, then you can practise your lines again for an hour. You should (try / will try) to get a good night's sleep, too.
Danny:	OK, Mum. Thanks.

B Practise the dialogue in **A** with a partner.

C Ask and answer the questions with a partner.

1 Has Danny studied enough for his Maths test? Explain.

2 Why does Danny's mum want him to get a good night's sleep?

3 Which do you think Danny should do first, study for his test or learn his lines? Explain.

4 Have you ever had to do two important things at the same time? What happened?

1
2
3
4
5
6
7
8
9

Get set.

 STEP 1 Cut out the cards on page 159 of your Activity Book.

 STEP 2 Lay out all the cards on your desk. Now you're ready to **Go!**

 Go!

A   Work with a partner. Look at the questions. You will use them to create two dialogues.

B   Create the first dialogue. Pupil A reads these questions and Pupil B chooses five responses from the cutouts. Read the dialogue aloud.

C   Switch roles and create the second dialogue. The new Pupil A reads these questions and the new Pupil B answers the questions with the remaining cutouts.

Pupil A
1 Have you chosen the topic of your project yet?
2 Why did you choose that topic?
3 What do you need to do for the project?
4 Have you already started the project?
5 Do you need to buy anything for the project?

D   Now make up your own dialogue. Role play your dialogue in front of another pair.

Pupil A	Pupil B
You're the mum or dad of Pupil B. You want to know all about your son or daughter's project.	You're doing a project on a topic that you're really interested in. You've already started the project but you haven't finished yet.

5 Write about yourself in your notebook.

- Where do you live? How long have you lived there?
- How long have you been learning English?
- Which places have you visited in your country or city? When did you go there?
- If you learn English well, what will you be able to do in the future?
- If you go to university, what might you study there?

All About Me   Date:_____

_____

_____

How Well Do I Know It Now?

6 Look at page 52 and your notebook. Draw again.

A   Use a different colour.

B   Read and think.

I can start the next unit.

I can ask my teacher for help and then start the next unit.

I can practise and then start the next unit.

7 Rate this Checkpoint.

very easy   easy   hard   very hard   fun   OK   not fun

Units 1-3 Exam Preparation

Listen and draw lines. There is one example.

Emma   George   Harry   Sarah

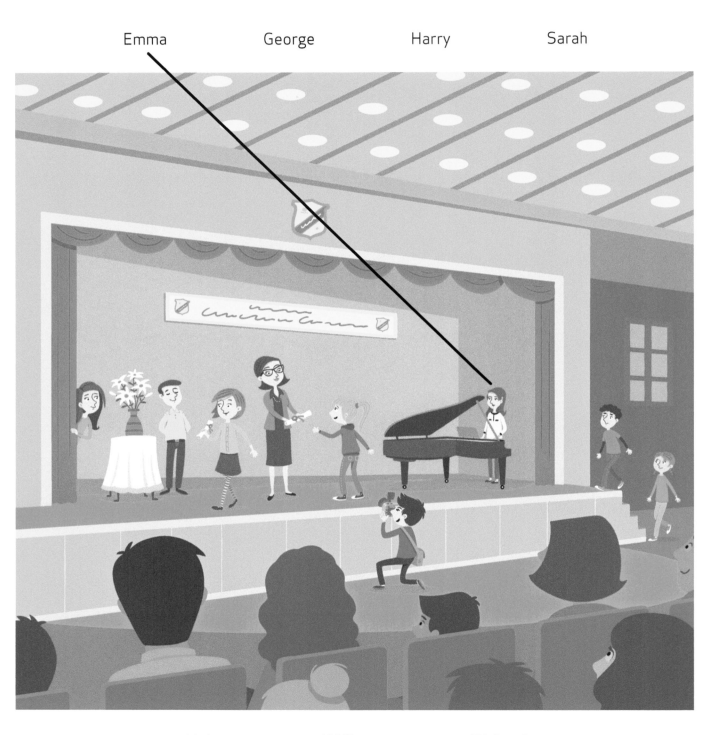

Helen   William   Richard

- Part B -

Lucy is talking to her friend, Alice. What does Alice say? Read the conversation and choose the best answer. Write a letter (A–H) for each answer. You do not need to use all the letters.

Example

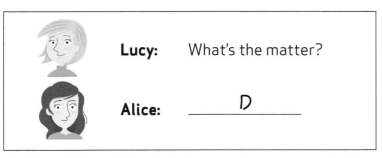

Lucy:	What's the matter?
Alice:	___D___

Questions

1

Lucy: Oh, no! Do you think someone has stolen it?

Alice: _____

2

Lucy: Is it a new phone?

Alice: _____

3

Lucy: Perhaps you should ring them.

Alice: _____

4

Lucy: OK. Look! What's that on the floor under your desk?

Alice: _____

5

Lucy: Well, I expect you dropped it or maybe it just fell out of your backpack.

Alice: _____

A I can't! If I tell them, I'll get into trouble again. Let's see if we can find it first.

B I don't believe it – my phone! How did it get there?

C I'm not sure. I had it in my backpack this morning.

D I've lost my mobile phone! **(Example)**

E You're right. I should be more careful!

F I haven't looked under the desk yet.

G I've only had this backpack for two weeks.

H Yes, it is! I've already lost one, so my parents will be really angry with me!

unit 4

DREAMS FOR THE FUTURE

56
1

Read the predictions made by John E. Watkins in the year 1900. Say which predictions you think came true. Then listen to check.

I, John E. Watkins, an American civil engineer, predict that in one hundred years from now...

1   Trains will travel at speeds of up to 240 kilometres per hour.

2   A man in the middle of the Atlantic Ocean will be talking to his family in Chicago. It'll be like his family is sitting next to him!

3   People will be buying ready-cooked meals.

4   People will be sending photographs from anywhere in the world. Photographs of major events from another continent will be in newspapers in an hour and they'll have the colours of nature.

5   People will be eating strawberries as big as apples! Raspberries and blackberries will also be big.

6   Americans will be taller by three to five centimetres.

57

2 Look at the list as you listen to two boys discussing their dreams for the future. Which topics do you hear them talking about?

DREAMS FOR THE FUTURE

I'll be working in my dream job.

I'll be running my own business.

I'll be living in another country.

I'll be married.

I'll be bringing up a family.

I'll be working in the music industry.

I'll be going on adventurous holidays.

I'll be speaking several foreign languages including English.

I'll be earning a good salary.

I'll be famous.

3 Imagine your life in twenty years. Look at the list in 2 and think about each statement. Which do you think you'll be doing?

4 Work with a partner. Ask and answer about what you'll be doing in twenty years.

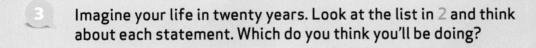
What will you be doing in twenty years?

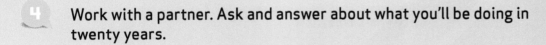
I'll be working in the music industry and earning a good salary.

THINK BIG What do you think the world will be like thirty years from now in terms of:
- education?
- transport?
- everyday life?

5 On futureme.org, people write to themselves in the future. MeToday has written three emails to her future self. Listen and read. How old will she be ten years from now?

futureme.org

TO MeToday@iMail2014.com
CC
SUBJECT Ten years from now

Dear FutureSelf:

It's 2014. I'm in my Year 7 English class. Ten years from now, I'll be studying at a big university. I'll probably have a lot of classmates from different parts of the country and the world. I won't be making much money yet so I'll be living in a small flat near the university to save money. But I know I'll be successful after I graduate.

MeToday

TO MeToday@iMail2014.com
CC
SUBJECT Thirty years from now

Dear FutureSelf:

It's 2014. Right now, I'm in Year 7. In thirty years, I'll be living in London and learning to speak another foreign language, probably Japanese. I'll be working in a beautiful office with a great view of the Thames and I'll hopefully be running my own business. I won't be bringing up a big family because I'll be working hard. It's OK. I won't work long hours all my life. I really want to have children, a dog and a cat, too.

MeToday

www.futureme.org

TO: MeToday@iMail2014.com

CC:

SUBJECT: Fifty years from now

Dear FutureSelf:

It's 2014. I'm twelve years old this year and I'm in Year 7. Wow, I'll be sixty-two years old fifty years from now! I'll probably be living back home in my country. I definitely won't be working. I'll be living in a small house, enjoying my retirement. My grandchildren will be visiting me often. We'll be taking rides in my flying sports car!

MeToday

READING COMPREHENSION

6 **What will MeToday be doing in the future? Find and compare with a partner.**

1 Find two things MeToday will be doing ten years from now.
Find one thing she won't be doing.

2 Find two things MeToday will be doing thirty years from now.
Find one thing she won't be doing.

3 Find two things MeToday will be doing fifty years from now.
Find one thing she won't be doing.

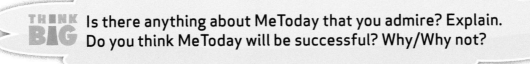

THINK BIG Is there anything about MeToday that you admire? Explain.
Do you think MeToday will be successful? Why/Why not?

Language in Action

60

7 Listen and read. Where will people be going on holiday in the future?

Lisa: I'll definitely buy a nice car when I grow up.

Gavin: A car? We'll probably be flying around in spaceships when we're older!

Lisa: You're such a dreamer.

Gavin: Well, maybe in <u>twenty or thirty</u> years.

Lisa: So, do you think we'll be taking a spaceship to work every day?

Gavin: Why not? I'll be living in <u>Tokyo</u> and working in <u>Madrid</u>.

Lisa: But the world is running out of oil. If there's no oil, how will we fly around in spaceships?

Gavin: People will discover a new source of fuel so we won't need oil.

Lisa: But if we've all got spaceships, travelling won't be exciting any more! Where will we go on holiday?

Gavin: Maybe we'll be <u>visiting other planets</u>!

8 Practise the dialogue in 7 with a partner. Change the underlined words.

61

9 Listen and match. Then complete the sentences. Use the correct form of the verb.

1 In 100 years, we'll 🤔 .

2 In twenty years, she'll 🤔 .

3 In fifteen years, he'll 🤔 .

4 In forty years, they'll 🤔 .

> live in
> read
> travel to
> work on

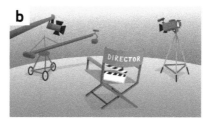

What **will** you **be doing** ten years from now?	I'**ll** definitely **be studying** at a big university.
Where **will** you **be living** in twenty years?	I probably **won't be living** in Europe.

Tip: Use the future continuous to talk about what you'll be doing in the future. For degrees of certainty (how likely something is), use either *definitely* or *probably*.

10 What will you or won't you be doing forty years from now? Make complete sentences. Use the future continuous of the verbs in brackets and definitely or probably.

1 (live in another country) 🔒

2 (run my own business) 🔒

3 (go on holidays on the moon) 🔒

4 (go on white-water rafting trips) 🔒

5 (teach chemistry at the university) 🔒

6 (make a big archaeological discovery) 🔒

Will you **be running** a business?	No, definitely not. I definitely **won't**…
	Yes, definitely. I definitely **will**…
	Probably not. I probably **won't**…
	Yes, probably. I probably **will**…

11 Make Yes/No questions about the future. Use the ideas below or your own ideas. Exchange your questions with a partner. Take turns with your partner to ask and answer your questions.

bring up a family

make huge scientific discoveries

live in a big city

earn good money

travel around the globe

make a difference to the world

work for an environmental organisation

act in films/on TV

Content Connection | Science and Technology

 12 Look at some new technologies. What are they? What do you know about them? Collect information with your class.

> artificial intelligence   driverless cars   laser surgery   nanotechnology
> smart glasses   virtual reality   3-D printing

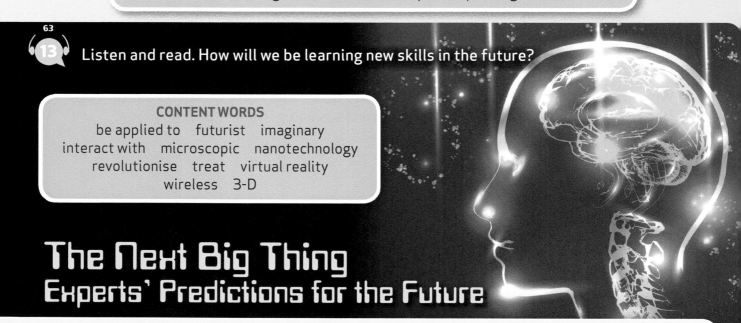

63

13 Listen and read. How will we be learning new skills in the future?

CONTENT WORDS
be applied to   futurist   imaginary
interact with   microscopic   nanotechnology
revolutionise   treat   virtual reality
wireless   3-D

The Next Big Thing
Experts' Predictions for the Future

1   Futurists are people whose job is to look ahead and help us plan for the future. Futurists can't say exactly what the future will be like, but they use their knowledge to say what will probably happen and what we can prepare ourselves for. How will we be learning fifty years from now? How will we treat illness? How will people be living and communicating? Let's take a look at three big things futurists are talking about today.

Virtual Reality

2   In a virtual-reality game, you, as a player, experience an imaginary world and interact with game characters as though you were part of that world. It doesn't have to be a game – the technology can be applied to other arenas, too. Imagine yourself in a virtual-reality school of the future, where you can socialise and learn with virtual people. You can be anywhere in the world and study at the school of your choice. Cool, don't you think? In order for this to happen, a 3-D image linked to your brain will make you feel as though you're actually in the classroom, interacting with your virtual teacher and virtual classmates.

Nanotechnology

3   Nanotechnology is the science of incredibly small things. As a unit of measure, a nanometre is one billionth of a metre! When something is nano size, it's so small it's invisible! With nanotechnology, we'll have microscopic computerised robots called nanobots. Because nanobots can be built into almost anything – even appliances – household chores will be easier. Nanobots could also be used to travel inside your body and treat problems and disease without expensive and painful operations.

Brain-to-Computer Communication

4   How about this for an amazing prediction: One day, everyone and everything will be linked through wireless technology. Nanocomputers will be in your system, so your brain, just like a computer, will be able to receive downloads and uploads. Would you like to learn a new language or how to tango? As soon as you think the thought, your brain will download the new language or the dance steps and you'll be learning them instantly!

5   All these new technologies promise to revolutionise the way we live and experience things. Now perhaps the big question is: are we ready for them?

64   Unit 4

14 **Look at** 13. **Read and say** yes, no **or** doesn't say.

1 Futurists can't predict what the future will definitely be like.

2 Virtual reality games are popular all over the world.

3 In a virtual-reality school, pupils can live in one country and study in another.

4 Nanotechnology could help us do household chores.

5 Nanobots could make operations more painful.

6 With brain-to-computer communication, robots will teach us to dance.

15 **Work with a partner. Match the technologies to their possible applications in the future. Which application do you think is the most important?**

1 Virtual reality   2 Nanotechnology   3 Brain-to-computer communication

a We'll be able to practise a foreign language with people in another country.

b We'll be curing disease by killing only diseased cells in our body.

c We'll be able to see live concerts anywhere in the world without leaving our home.

d We'll be learning things much faster without any effort.

e We'll be able to interact and spend time with friends and relatives who live far away.

f Household appliances will be more intelligent and efficient.

16 **Discuss these questions in groups. Collect ideas, then write about a future technology you find interesting.**

1 Which future technology in the article is the most exciting in your opinion? Why?

2 What other applications can you think of for the technology?

3 Are there any disadvantages of these applications?

THINK BIG If you could learn something by uploading it to your brain instantly, what would you like to learn? Why? Can you think of any bad things about the technologies in the article?

65

 Read the predictions and guess the dates. Then listen and check your answers.

Four predictions that didn't come true!

a When Henry Ford opened the first Ford car factory in ¹ , the president of the bank didn't want to lend him money. The bank president thought that cars were a silly invention. He said that people would always prefer horses to cars.

b The French brothers Auguste and Louis Lumiere invented the cinema in Paris in ² . But they said that films wouldn't be popular. They said that cinema was an invention without a future!

c Twelve publishers refused to publish the first *Harry Potter* book! In ³ , a publisher told author JK Rowling that children wouldn't like Harry Potter. This publisher said that children weren't interested in witches and wizards any more. JK Rowling said she would find another publisher.

d In ⁴ , a record company boss said that he didn't like the sound of a group of musicians from Liverpool. He said that the group would definitely fail, because people didn't like four-piece bands with guitars! A few years later, the Beatles were the most successful band in the world.

18 **Look at** 17 **and complete.**

"Cars **are** a silly invention."	The president **said that** cars ¹ a silly invention.
"People **will always prefer** horses to cars."	The president **said that** people ² horses to cars.
"Films **won't be** popular."	The Lumière brothers **said that** films ³ popular.
Tip: Use **said** or **said that** to report speech: He **said** (**that**) he didn't believe me.	

19 **Look at** 17 **and** 18. **Complete their actual words.**

1 The Lumiere brothers: "Cinema an invention without a future."

2 The bank president: "Cars are a silly invention. People horses to cars."

3 JK Rowling: "I another publisher."

4 The record company boss: "The group ."

5 The publisher: "Children *Harry Potter*. They aren't interested in witches and wizards any more."

20 What did they say? Read, match and report the speech. Follow the example.

| I'm a scientist! | I'll be late. | They won't be very popular. |

| I'll do it later. | We are at the beach. | I'm sure it'll rain. |

1 **A:** It's 8 p.m. and David isn't here. Where is he?

  B: Don't worry. He said he _would be late_ .

2 **A:** Erol has some really silly ideas.

  B: Yes. He said that he ? a scientist!

3 **A:** Jenny's room is messy. Why hasn't she tidied it?

  B: She said she ? .

4 **A:** Where are Mehmet and Anna?

  B: Well, they said they ? .

5 **A:** Everyone around the world knows Harry Potter.

  B: Yes, and one publisher said the books ? !

6 **A:** This is really bad weather!

  B: Yeah. My dad said that he ? .

21 Work in groups. Look at the instructions and play a game.

First write four things:

1 something that you will probably do next week

2 something that you probably will not do next week

3 something that you like

4 something that you don't like

Take turns in the group. Say one thing from your list.

> I'll probably go to the shopping centre next week.

Now report the sentences. Correct mistakes about things you said.

> Ana said that she would probably go to the cinema next week.

> No, I said that I would probably go to the shopping centre next week!

The Future Forum

Subject: Future predictions: what do you think?

On 12ᵗʰ January, Rick wrote:
In the world of ideas for the future, we kids have some amazing ideas. Because we're young, we've got a fresher outlook on life than adults. And in some cases, kids' predictions, especially about technology, have already turned out to be true. I found some old videos on the Internet from the 1990s showing children predicting amazing things they didn't have yet, including smartphone technology and the modern Internet. But kids also predict other things, like peace and harmony. I hope they're right about those! What do you think the future will be like? Write and let me know, so I can get ready!

Comments:

I think people around the world will be living happily. There won't be any wars between countries or among people of the same country. We'll learn to accept and help each other. Everyone will have food and shelter. People will be enjoying life because they won't have to worry about having a roof over their heads or having enough to eat.
Lisa, Australia

22 **Look at the questions. Answer with a partner, then share your ideas with the class.**

1 What are some big problems in the world today?

2 Do you think we'll be able to solve these problems in the future?

3 Do you think life will be easier or more difficult in the future?

23 **Read the web forum quickly. Match one main topic and one detail to each person.**

1 Lisa   **2** Rajeesh   **3** Kat   **4** Shen   **5** Anashe

TOPICS		DETAILS	
a	time travel	**f**	We'll be able to see ourselves and our family at different ages.
b	world peace	**g**	We won't need to do any boring jobs.
c	space travel	**h**	There won't be any wars or hunger.
d	the environment	**i**	People will come to Earth easily by shuttle.
e	robots	**j**	There won't be pollution and the environment will be safe.

Hi from India! I think nanobots and nanopets will be living with us. We won't have to do anything. Cool! Our nanobots will move exactly like us and do all our manual work for us. They'll be cleaning our house and doing our shopping and cooking. They'll even play games with us!
Rajeesh, India

People, no matter what their skin colour, gender, culture or religion is, will be co-existing harmoniously together. We'll all be citizens of the Earth and we'll be taking good care of our planet. The environment will be safe to live in. Plants and animals won't be in danger. In fact, we'll develop the technology to bring back animals that have already become extinct.
Kat, USA

There will be a time machine that will show us what we'll look like in the future. We'll be able to use the time machine to see the past, too – like what our parents and grandparents looked like when they were young.
Shen, China

In the future, there will be more space travel. We'll be using space shuttles in the same way we use buses now. People may choose to have their home on the moon and catch the shuttle to Earth every morning to go to work.
Anashe, South Africa

66

24 Listen and read. Choose the correct words.

1 Kids have a (less positive/more open) view of the world than adults.

2 In the 1990s, children were already (using/talking about) smartphones and the modern Internet.

3 Lisa predicts that there will be no (hunger/worries) in the future.

4 Rajeesh believes that we won't have to (go to work/do housework) in the future.

5 Kat says that there will be (fewer/more) kinds of plants and animals than there are now.

6 Shen thinks we'll be able to (travel in time/stay young).

25 Match the sentence halves to find some important global issues today.

1 One out of six children in developing countries	a they haven't got good healthcare.
2 Almost a billion people in the world can't	b read or write.
3 Many big cities near the sea	c drinking water.
4 In poor countries, people become ill because	d hasn't got enough food to eat.
5 Reports say that 11% of people in the world haven't got fresh	e are threatened because the sea level is rising.

26 Look at 25. Write a short prediction about one of the issues in the future. Use the web forum to help you. Collect your class predictions on a poster or website.

27 With a partner, read these two emails and decide which is formal and which is informal. Discuss the differences with your partner.

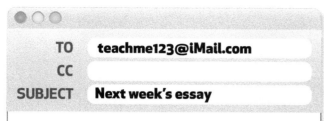

TO	teachme123@iMail.com
CC	
SUBJECT	Next week's essay

Dear Ms Priscott,
I'll be working on next week's essay this weekend because I've got play rehearsals all week but I need more information about it.
I've got some questions:
• What type of essay will we be writing?
• I'm planning to write about future technology. Is this topic OK?
• What is the deadline for the essay?
Thank you for your help.
Thomas Brown

TO	howcoolisit1@iMail.com
CC	
SUBJECT	This weekend

Hey Leo,
Any plans 4 tomorrow? Wanna hang out at my house? I'm staying home all day coz ive got to babysit my little sister. Wanna do homework together?
Got the new video game, btw. It's brilliant!
Just text me b4 u come over. OK? CU soon.
Thomas

28 Write two emails: one to a teacher and one to a friend.

Formal

TO	
CC	
SUBJECT	

Dear ?

Informal

TO	
CC	
SUBJECT	

Hey ?

 THINK BIG How can thinking about the past help you make better decisions in the present? Do you think it's good or bad to be thinking about and making plans for the future? Why/Why not?

29 Many young people don't think too much about the future. But they should. Read these statements. Think of a response to each one.

> Why do I have to learn English? I don't plan on living abroad so I don't need it.

?

> My parents own a business. I don't need to finish school because I'll be running the business when I'm old enough.

?

> Me? Learn how to do household chores? I don't think so! I'll have maids at home so I won't be doing any chores in the future.

?

PROJECT

 30 Make a FutureSelf book. Write a letter to yourself fifteen, thirty, even fifty years from now! Make a class book.

Dear FutureSelf,

Today is 4ᵗʰ January, 2014 and I'm in

Year 7. Fifteen years from now, I'll be living

on a tropical island. I'll be teaching at a

school there and living near the beach. I

won't be married or have children yet. I'll be...

31 Listen, read and repeat. *68*

1 eat**s**   **2** sing**s**   **3** wash**es**

 32 Listen and blend the sounds. *69*

1 c-oo-k-s   cooks   **2** r-u-n-s   runs
3 w-a-tch-es   watches   **4** s-l-ee-p-s   sleeps
5 s-w-i-m-s   swims   **6** d-a-n-c-es   dances

 33 Listen and chant. *70*

> Sol swims in the summer,
> He cooks in the winter,
> He dances on Fridays,
> He sings in the shower
> And he sleeps for hours!

34 Create class surveys.

1 Work in groups. Brainstorm a list of predictions.

2 Choose a group leader. The group leader conducts a class survey about one of your predictions.

> Will you be working in the fashion industry in thirty years?

> Yeah, I probably will be. I'm interested in designing clothes and I love art.

3 As a group, add up the results and create a graph. Then present your graph to the class.

> In our class, 15 out of 30 pupils think they definitely won't be working in the fashion industry.

35 Use the words in the box to complete the expressions.

> a business   a family   a foreign language   a good salary   adventurous holidays
> children   in a dream job   in a nice office   in another country

1 run ?

2 work ?

3 earn ?

4 bring up ?

5 go on ?

6 speak ?

36 In your notebook, write four sentences about what four of your classmates will be doing in the future. You can use the expressions in 35 plus probably or definitely.

37 In your notebook, write answers to the questions. Use complete sentences.

1 What will you probably be doing tonight at 7:20?

2 What will you be doing this time next year?

3 Will you be travelling with friends ten years from now? Why/Why not?

4 What will you definitely not be doing in the future?

5 Will you be bringing up a family fifteen years from now?

6 What will you be doing forty years from now?

7 Will you be earning a lot of money twenty years from now?

8 Will you be travelling in space fifty years from now?

38 Work with a partner. Role play the actual dialogue.

Ramon said he was very excited about his project's award. Mr Hill said that Ramon would be more excited after he heard the rest of the news. He said that Ramon wouldn't only get an award for his project. He said that he would also present the project to the School Science Competition! Ramon said that that was great news. He said that he was a bit anxious but he was sure he would try his best.

I Can

- **talk about and make predictions about the future.**
- **talk about levels of certainty.**
- **report actual speech.**

unit 5

IF I COULD FLY...

1 Listen and read about ideas that could change our lives. Discuss the questions in small groups. Then share your favourite idea with the class.

Now You See Me – Now You Don't!

In the Harry Potter films, Harry puts on a cloak that makes him invisible. When he does that, nobody can see him! Have you ever wished that you could be invisible? If so, you may get your wish sooner than you think. Scientists have been working on bending light around objects to make them hard to see. Think about it. If you could become invisible, what would you do?

Time After Time

People have always thought about travelling to a different time period. What about you? Would you like to go back to mediaeval times and meet a real knight? Or would you like to see what the future will be like in 100 years? Maybe someday you'll be able to do this! If you could travel through time, what time period and place would you visit? Why?

It's a Bird! It's a Plane! It's a... Car?

Did you know that flying cars already exist? This vehicle's got four wheels and wings that fold up. You can drive it on the road. And you can also open up the wings and fly in the air! Would you like to have a flying car? What would you use it for?

2 Some pupils are talking about things they could do if they had one of the super powers in the box. Listen and match.

> superhuman strength   the ability to become invisible
> the ability to fly   the ability to read people's minds
> the ability to run at lightning speed   the ability to travel through time

If you could have one super power, what would it be?

If I had this super power...

1

I know what super power I'd want!

2

There are so many things I could do...

3

I think I'd choose...

4

I'd want to have...

5

3 Work with a partner. Talk about super powers.

If you could have one super power, what would it be?

I'd want the ability to read people's minds.

THINK BIG What other super powers can you think of that could be useful to people? Do you think any of them could become reality? Why/Why not?

73

4 Listen and read. What's wrong with Captain Allsafe?

CAPTAIN ALLSAFE TO THE RESCUE!

by Buster Marone

READING COMPREHENSION

5 Number the events from the story in the order they happened.

a Captain Allsafe ties up a 'dinosaur'.

b Captain Allsafe sees a 'fire' and blows it out.

c Captain Allsafe sees smoke. He throws water and puts out the 'fire', pouring water onto the barbecue!

d Captain Allsafe is flying over the city and everything seems calm and quiet.

e Captain Allsafe hears children screaming.

f Captain Allsafe says that maybe he should go on a holiday.

g A woman brings out a birthday cake.

 Why doesn't Captain Allsafe want to go on holiday? If you were Captain Allsafe, would you go on holiday? Why? If you could give Captain Allsafe some advice, what would you tell him?

6 Listen and read. What would Ben and Alexa do if they had a certain super power?

Ben: I'm reading about this guy who can make objects move just by thinking about them. Isn't that cool?

Alexa: That's very cool. I wish I could do that.

Ben: Yeah? If you could move things with your mind, what would you do?

Alexa: I'd clean up my room – hands-free, no physical effort.

Ben: You're thinking too small, Alexa. If I had that power, I'd move our town closer to the beach.

Alexa: Oh! I like that. Then we could move all our friends' houses next to our houses.

Ben: Now you're getting the idea.

7 Practise the dialogue in 6 with a partner.

8 Listen and match. What would each person do? Make complete sentences.

> go back in time   have any job
> have anything to eat   talk to animals

1 If Maya could ❓, she'd ❓.   **2** If Kelly could ❓, she'd ❓.
3 If Luke could ❓, he'd ❓.   **4** If Daniel could ❓, he'd ❓.

if clause	result clause
If I **were** you,	**I'd choose** something else.
If he **made** his bed every day,	his mum **would be** happy.
If she **could have** one super power,	she**'d breathe** underwater.

Tip: Use *if* to talk about situations that are not true or contrary to fact. For example: *If I were you = I'm not you.*

9 Choose the correct verbs to complete the sentences.

1 If I (could breathe/would breathe) underwater, I (will explore/would explore) the bottom of the sea.

2 If I (owned/will own) a horse, I (would ride/will ride) it every day.

3 If you (ate/will eat) healthier food, you (are going to be/would be) stronger.

4 If we (can read/could read) people's minds, we (knew/would know) when they were lying.

If you **didn't have to go** to school, what **would** you **do** every day?	If I **didn't have to go** to school, I **would stay** home and **listen** to music all day.
If you **could go** anywhere, where **would** you **go**?	If I **could go** anywhere, I**'d go** to Paris.

10 Choose phrases from the box to complete the questions. Then answer the questions for you. Make complete sentences.

> who would you like to meet?
> whose mind would you read?
> when would you travel to?
> where else would you be now?
> what would you dream about?

1 If you could be in two places at the same time, ❓
   Answer: ❓

2 If you could meet a TV or film star, ❓
   Answer: ❓

3 If you could make up your own dreams, ❓
   Answer: ❓

4 If you could read people's minds, ❓
   Answer: ❓

5 If you could travel through time, ❓
   Answer: ❓

Look at the questions. Answer with a partner, then share your ideas with the class.

Who's your favourite superhero?

What special powers has he/she got?

 Read and put sentences a–d **in the correct place. Then listen and check your answers.**

a This would really be a digital world!

b We'll have to invent new, more exciting superheroes!

c Maybe we'll see skyscraper climbing as an Olympic sport one day!

d It would certainly make texting in class easier!

> **CONTENT WORDS**
>
> activate   adhesive   electrode   endless   experiment   fascinating
> gecko   gesture   interact   skyscraper   spell out   work on

Super Power or Super Science?

1 People have always found super powers fascinating. We love watching films about superheroes because they can do things that humans can't. Or can we? Every year, engineers create new technologies that people couldn't even imagine in the past. Here are three surprising things that scientists are already working on.

2 Have you ever seen a gecko climb up a wall and wondered why it doesn't fall off? Geckos have got very sticky feet, which stop them slipping off the wall. If a human could climb like a gecko, it would seem like a super power. Scientists are experimenting with plastic to make an adhesive (a kind of glue) that will let humans climb up walls… and they are close to succeeding! [1]

3 How would you like to be able to tweet without using a keyboard? Believe it or not, there's a scientist who's trying to make this possible! His idea uses a cap with electrodes. While wearing the cap, he concentrates on one letter at a time, spelling out his message on a computer screen! He's able to tweet eight letters a minute. But in the future, who knows? [2]

4 Mark Rolston, a computer designer, thinks that computers as we know them – a monitor, a keyboard and speakers – limit us. He believes that we need to start thinking that the computer is the room we're in. Imagine, for example, being able to watch the news on the kitchen table, make a video call on your fridge and read a recipe on the wall above your cooker, activating the computer using only your voice or gestures. [3]

5 It seems that the future offers endless possibilities. One day we might be climbing buildings like Spider-Man or interacting with others by thought alone. The only problem? [4]

13 Look at 12. Read and complete the sentences with phrases from the text.

1 Engineers are constantly making new things that people 😕.

2 Geckos don't slip off the wall because they 😕.

3 One scientist can tweet with his brain when he wears 😕.

4 Mark Rolston believes we should think that 😕.

5 According to Mark Rolston, we should be able to see news programs 😕.

6 The future doesn't seem to limit technology – there are 😕.

14 Work in groups. Answer the questions.

1 Which of the 'super powers' in the text would be the most useful to you? Why?

2 How is technology changing now? Think about televisions, computers and smartphones. Compare them to three years ago.

15 Look at six things that give us 'super powers', then read about the superheroes. Match the things to the superheroes, then write the super power. Follow the example.

1 a whistle that copies bird sounds
   Wonder Woman — can communicate with animals

2 a powerful skin cream for cuts and injuries 😕

3 an oxygen mask and tank for diving 😕

4 vitamins and minerals to help people stay young 😕

5 a powerful motorbike 😕

6 a powerful hearing aid 😕

WONDER WOMAN

She's got the powers of super strength and speed. She can fly and she can communicate with animals.

THE HULK

His strength is incredible – he can create thunder-like force when he claps his hands, he can jump for miles, he heals instantly and he can breathe under water.

WOLVERINE

He can heal from any injury very fast, he ages very slowly, he can't be poisoned and he's got long claws, super hearing and super sight.

80

16 Listen and read. Note your answers to the personality quiz, then check your score. What are most people in your class like?

What are you really like?

Choose one answer each time.

• •

1 Complete this sentence: If I won a lot of money, ...

a I'd be able to give a few euros to my sister/brother/best friend.

b I could spend it all on me!

c I'd definitely give half to charity.

2 Which piece of advice do you like best?

a "If I were you, I'd try to make friends all through your life."

b "The most important thing in life is money."

c "We should all try to make the world a better place."

3 What would you do if you found €20 in the street?

a I might take my friend out for a pizza.

b I'd go shopping and buy myself new stuff.

c I'd give it to a homeless person.

4 Which idea do you like best?

a If I had wings and could fly, I could give rides to my friends!

b If I had super powers, I might become extremely rich.

c If I could go back to the past, I'd be able to stop all wars before they started.

How did you score?

Mostly 'a's: you are loyal to your friends and family
Mostly 'b's: you think money is very important
Mostly 'c's: you always think about other people first

 17 Look at 16 and complete.

if clause	result clause
If I **won** a lot of money,	I ¹🎁 a few euros to my sister.
If I **were** you,	I ²🎁 to make friends all through my life.
If I **could** fly,	I ³🎁 rides to my friends.
If I **had** super powers,	I ⁴🎁 extremely rich.

Tip: Use **might** (**not**) when you aren't sure what will happen.
Use **could** or **would be able to** to talk about a conditional ability:
If I had a lot of money, I **could/would be able to** buy a car.

18 **Match.**

1 If I had a big garden,
2 If I won a million euros,
3 What would you be
4 If more people used bicycles,
5 What would you do if
6 If I were you,

a you turned into a mouse?
b I'd stop daydreaming and do some work!
c I might build a tree house.
d there might be less pollution.
e if you could choose any job in the world?
f I might give half of it to charity.

19 **Read and choose the correct words.**

1 If I were invisible, I (would be able to/can) go to the cinema without paying!
2 What (do/would) you say if you met Einstein?
3 If you could go back in time, you (might/will) meet Christopher Columbus.
4 If you (can/could) be a superhero, which one (did/would) you choose to be?
5 Where (do/would) you go first, if you (can/could) fly?
6 If I (would be/were) you, I (didn't/wouldn't) worry about the future.

20 **Read and complete these sentences for you.**

1 If I could be any animal, I'd be a ?.
2 If I could choose a superpower, I'd choose ?.
3 If I could choose any career, I'd choose to be ?.
4 If I could live anywhere in the world, I might live in ?.
5 If I were a fly/a spider/a horse/a bird, ?.
6 If I were invisible, I could ?

21 **Look at** 20. **Work in groups. Take turns saying one of your sentences. Other people in your group say what might happen.**

If I were invisible, I could go to all the big pop concerts without a ticket.

If you were invisible and went to a pop concert, someone might walk over you!

If I could be any animal, I'd be a horse.

If you were a horse, somebody really heavy might sit on you and hurt your back!

Superheroes from Different Cultures

1 In 1938, a man in a red cape and a blue costume appeared in an action comic for the first time. He was strong enough to lift a car and he could fly. He was the first superhero – Superman. He went on to become famous all over the world.

2 Every superhero has got a story. Generally, they've suffered a trauma. Batman, for example, lost his family and wants to save people from similar situations. Something often happens to them accidentally to give them their super power, too. Spider-Man is bitten by a spider at a science exhibit, which turns him into a human spider. Also, heroes have often got a 'normal' daily life. In everyday life, Superman is a journalist.

3 Although many superheroes originated in the USA, there are many other countries with their own superheroes. Japan, which has got the largest comic book industry in the world (called manga), has got many heroes. Mexican writers started creating their own native heroes in the 1990s and in India, comic books have been around for the last 50 years. Here are some popular examples.

22 **Work with a partner. Do you know your superheroes? Do this quick superhero quiz.**

1 In everyday life, Superman is…

a a doctor.   b a journalist.   c a pilot.

2 Superman's clothes are…

a blue and yellow.   b red and yellow.   c blue and red.

3 Spider-Man got his super powers after…

a he looked after spiders when he was young.   b an operation on a spider went wrong.   c he was bitten by a spider.

4 When Batman was a child, …

a he lost his mother and father.   b he lived on a different planet.   c he ate something that gave him super powers.

5 What is another name for Japanese comic art?

a manga   b tanka   c anime

23 **Read the article quickly and check your answers. Which other superheroes does the article describe?**

4 Cat Girl Nuku Nuku – Japan

In everyday life, this hero is called Atsuko 'Nuku Nuku' Natsume. She's an android with a cat's brain but she goes to school every day with her 'brother', Ryunosuke. Nuku Nuku is a highly advanced android with the reflexes and senses of a cat. She's also got superhuman strength.

5 Meteorix – Mexico

He goes to school, where he's known as Aldo.
He's got superhuman strength and can throw bolts of blue lightning. He gained his super powers when he swallowed a piece of meteorite which fell to Earth. His mission is to protect Mexico City from dangerous criminals.

6 Bantul the Great – India

Bantul just does odd jobs. If he didn't have his super powers, he might not get in trouble, but he often does. He looks after two mischievous school boys. He's got a really big appetite and sometimes he eats a whole whale for breakfast! Bantul is incredibly strong. He could stop a train if he stood in front of it. He can move things just by blowing air out of his mouth, and bullets can't hurt him.

 24 **Listen and read. Choose the correct words.**
81

1 Superman first appeared in (a blue cape/1938).

2 Every superhero has (lost someone they love/experienced a problem in their life).

3 Most superheroes (are different in normal life/save people every day).

4 (The USA/Japan) produces the most comic books in the world.

5 India has had a comic book industry (since the 1990s/for the last 50 years).

25 **Read again and say** Nuku Nuku, Meteorix or Bantul.

1 needs a lot of food

2 has got animal powers

3 changed after eating something

4 goes to school

5 sometimes gets into trouble

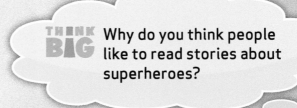

THINK BIG Why do you think people like to read stories about superheroes?

26 Choose a superhero who's well known in your country. Write an entry for a Superhero fact file. Include information about their childhood and how they got their super powers.

27 Create and describe a superhero character of your own. Use the questions to help you. Take notes and discuss with a partner.

- What are your character's superhero and everyday names?
- What is his or her everyday occupation?
- What is his or her country of origin?
- In what time period does your character live?
- What does he or she look like?
- Has he or she got a family? If so, describe each member.
- What are your character's super powers?
- What is your character's mission?

28 Use your answers in 27 to copy and make a card about your character in your notebook. Draw a picture.

Superhero name: ?

Everyday name: ?

Everyday occupation: ?

Country of origin: ?

Time period: ?

Description: ?

Family: ?

Super powers: ?

Mission: ?

29 Swap and talk about your superhero cards. Which ones do you like best?

30 In real life, no one has got super powers. But there have been some super achievements. Discuss them with a partner and decide which three are the greatest.

We have…

1 visited the moon.

3 invented hot-air balloons and aeroplanes.

5 found ways to prevent and cure many diseases.

7 created systems that bring clean water into homes.

2 invented alphabets and writing.

4 mapped the stars.

6 learnt how to use electricity.

8 invented the internet.

31 Make a list of three positive steps you could take to help with the future of our world. Discuss them with a partner and choose the best one.

> If I could do three things to help improve the world, I would… ?

THINK BIG Why is it important to think about the future of the world now? What can you do to help people start thinking about our world's future?

> If I could do one thing, I'd help clean up our oceans and seas!

PROJECT

32 Create a page for a class book about positive steps for the future. Share your page with the class.

1 Create a page for your best positive step for the future from 31.

2 Draw pictures or use pictures from magazines to illustrate it.

3 Show your page and talk about why the step is important.

Protect Our Oceans

Oceans make up 70% of our Earth

33 Listen, read and repeat.

1 walked   2 cleaned   3 painted

34 Listen and blend the sounds.

1 w-a-tch-ed   watched   2 cl-i-mb-ed   climbed

3 w-a-n-t-ed   wanted   4 l-oo-k-ed   looked

5 c-a-ll-ed   called   6 e-n-d-ed   ended

35 Listen and chant.

> We walked in the jungle
> And we climbed trees
> Which ended in the sky!
> We looked at birds
> And we wanted to fly!

36 Conduct an interview.

> act in a film with any actor   become invisible
> have any kind of pet   live anywhere
> move things with your mind   sing with any musician or band
> travel anywhere in the world

1 Choose a classmate to interview.

2 Ask him/her questions using the ideas in the box. Note down their answers.

If you could travel anywhere in the world, where would you go?

I'd go to Argentina. I'd love to see the penguins!

If he could travel anywhere in the world, he'd go to Argentina to see the penguins.

37 Complete the sentences with the correct phrases from the box.

> be invisible   fly   had superhuman strength
> read my mind   run at lightning speed   travel through time

1 If you could ?, you'd know what I'm thinking right now.

2 I wish I could ? right now. I don't want anyone to see me.

3 In the film, the hero ? so he lifted the car off the railway track.

4 In the story, the character could go back to the past. He could ?.

5 He's a gold medallist in athletics. He can practically ?!

6 If we could ?, we wouldn't need to spend money on plane tickets!

 38 Complete the sentences using the words or phrases in brackets and your own information. Use would, might (not), could and would be able to.

1 (fly)
If I ?, I ?.

2 (read people's minds)
If I ?, I ?.

3 (become invisible)
If I ?, I ?.

4 (be a scientist)
If I ?, I ?.

5 (have superhuman strength)
If I ?, I ?.

6 (be older)
If I ?, I ?.

7 (run at lightning speed)
If I ?, I ?.

8 (meet someone from the past)
If I ?, I ?.

9 (travel to the future)
If I ?, I ?.

10 (be a famous person for a day)
If I ?, I ?.

I Can

- **talk about what I would, could and might do in different situations.**

- **answer questions about unreal situations.**

THE COOLEST SCHOOL SUBJECTS

86

1 Read. Match what you learn to the school subject where you learn it. Listen to check.

Things we learn about	School subject
1 Shakespeare	a Maths
2 democracy	b P.E.
3 sloths and pitcher plants	c English
4 sports and athletics	d Literature
5 vocabulary and grammar	e Science: Biology
6 prime numbers	f Social Science
7 murals	g Art

2 Look at the list. Find the school subjects you have and add two more. Then discuss the questions with a partner.

- Which of these subjects is your favourite? Why?
- Name some things you learn about in this subject.
- Which subject is the most difficult for you? Why?

Maths	P.E.
English	Science
Social Science	Art
Literature	?

3 Listen. A group of pupils is putting on a game show. Copy the chart and complete it as you listen.

artist   democracy   mammal   meat-eating plant
Olympic Games   playwright   prime numbers   speakers of English

	What each question is about	School subject
1	the earliest ❔	❔
2	the greatest ❔	❔
3	the earliest form of ❔	❔
4	the ten smallest ❔	❔
5	the slowest ❔	❔
6	the biggest ❔	❔
7	the most ❔	❔
8	Mexico's greatest mural ❔	❔

4 Have your own game show! Work in small groups. Follow the steps.

1 Choose your roles: Assign a game show host and contestants.

2 The host should use his/her notes from the chart above to ask the contestants questions.

3 See who gets the most correct answers.

4 Having fun? Take turns being the host. Use other information from your own lessons to ask more questions.

This is a Social Science question. Ready? Where were the earliest Olympic Games held?

They were held in Greece!

THINK BIG Which three school subjects do you think are the most important? Why?

88

5 Listen and read. What decision did Paris have to make?

The Judgment of Paris

A GREEK MYTH

retold by *Sam Riley*

Once upon a time, the Greek goddesses Hera, Aphrodite and Athena were arguing about who among the three of them was the fairest – or the most beautiful – goddess on Mount Olympus. They needed some help so they chose Paris, the youngest son of King Priam of Troy, to be the judge. Of course, it wasn't a very objective process. All three goddesses offered Paris the best gift they could offer in order to make Paris decide in their favour. Athena, the Greek goddess of wisdom and knowledge, offered Paris wisdom; Hera, the wife of Zeus, offered him power. But in Paris's mind, Aphrodite, the goddess of love and beauty, gave the best offer of all: she would give Paris the most beautiful woman in the world. So Paris made his decision: The fairest goddess on Mount Olympus was Aphrodite. He gave her a golden apple which had this inscription: 'To the fairest'.

But Aphrodite didn't tell Paris that there was a problem with her offer. As it turned out, the most beautiful woman in the world wasn't free. Helen, Queen of Sparta, was the most beautiful woman in the world at the time and King Menelaus was her husband. But a promise is a promise. Besides, Aphrodite was the goddess of love; with her power, she could make anyone fall in love.

So Aphrodite sent Paris to Sparta, where King Menelaus and Queen Helen welcomed him. Aphrodite kept her promise. She made Helen fall in love with Paris and the two ran away to Troy, where Paris lived. King Menelaus was, of course, furious. He asked all the best Greek warriors to help him get Helen back. In response, more than a thousand Greek ships and a hundred thousand Greek soldiers set sail for Troy. And that was how the Trojan War began.

READING COMPREHENSION

6 **What did the goddesses offer to Paris to make him judge in their favour?**

1 Athena

2 Hera

3 Aphrodite

7 **Answer the questions.**

1 Whose offer did Paris accept?

2 What was the problem with Aphrodite's offer?

3 How did Aphrodite keep her promise to Paris?

4 How did the Trojan war begin?

THINK BIG If you were Paris, would you agree to be the judge of this contest? Why/Why not? Whose gift would you accept? Why? What does Paris' choice show about him as a person?

8 Listen and read. What is Angela going to do for her Literature assignment?

Dad: Hi, Angela. You look happy. It seems like you've been enjoying school these days.

Angela: I have been. We've been reading a lot of Greek myths and legends in my Literature class. They're really great.

Dad: This may surprise you but I love myths and legends, too.

Angela: Do you? Well, maybe you can give me some advice. Our teacher wants us to write a play based on a myth.

Dad: That sounds like fun. How about 'Pandora's Box'?

Angela: I know that one. Pandora opens a beautiful clay box that she wasn't supposed to open and evil escapes into the world. That one's a little depressing.

Dad: Good point. Maybe you could do 'The Judgment of Paris'.

Angela: Hmm... that sounds familiar. What's it about?

Dad: I'll tell you the story...

9 Practise the dialogue in 8 with a partner.

10 Listen and match. Then complete the sentences. Include most or least and an adjective from the box.

> amazing   difficult
> endangered   favourite

1 He's looking for the ❓ of the play.

2 You can do the ❓ with these!

3 This is one of the ❓ in the world.

4 This is her ❓ in the school year.

a

b

c

d

> China's got **more** speakers of English **than** the USA.
>
> I've got **fewer** school subjects **than** my brother.
>
> Teachers in Finland give **less** homework **than** teachers in the UK.
>
> **Tip:** Use *fewer* with countable things. Use *less* with amounts that aren't countable.

11 **Complete these facts about plants and animals. Use** more, fewer **and** less.

1 Sloths spend ❓ time doing any form of activity than most animals. Most of their time is spent sleeping or just hanging out – upside down!

2 There are ❓ fish than dogs and cats as pets in the UK. There are approximately 40 million fish in tanks and ponds and 17 million pet dogs and cats in the UK.

3 The panda spends ❓ time sleeping than eating. Pandas eat bamboo for 14 to 16 hours a day!

4 Trees use carbon dioxide to make food. The ❓ trees there are, the ❓ carbon dioxide in the atmosphere.

> The Amazon rainforest has got **the most** species of plants and animals on Earth.
>
> Germany and Switzerland have got **the fewest** pet dogs per capita.
>
> Which country has got **the least** amount of air pollution?

12 **Complete the text with** the fewest, the least **or** the most.

Antarctica is full of extremes. It is ¹❓ remote region on Earth. There are no permanent residents. This makes Antarctica ²❓ populated continent on the planet. In spite of the snowy conditions, Antarctica is actually considered a desert. It's got ³❓ amount of rainfall of any place in the world. Not surprisingly, Antarctica has got ⁴❓ flowering plants of any other continent. The McMurdo Dry Valleys, one of ⁵❓ extreme desert regions in the world, is the largest ice-free region in Antarctica.

13 Each creature in the box has got a special ability. What is the ability? How is it used? What else do you know about these creatures? Collect information with your class.

> a chameleon   a flea   a leopard   a starfish

94

14 Listen and read the article. Which special abilities does it describe?

> **CONTENT WORDS**
> absorb   adapt   blink   break down   carnivore   digest   give birth
> herbivore   infection   injure   nectar   nutrients   protein   rays   slippery

Biology: The Weirdest Living Things

1   Over time, animals on our planet have developed so that they can survive in the best way possible. Some animals have got rare abilities that make them particularly interesting. Read on to find out about three of them.

2   **Sloths** are the slowest creatures on Earth. Everything they do is slow. They eat slowly, blink slowly and move slowly. They're so slow that they need a month to move one kilometre! They're also the sleepiest animals alive; they sleep up to twenty hours a day! They eat fruit and leaves and because they're so slow and sleepy, they burn energy very slowly. Sloths live in trees in the rainforests of South and Central America. Because they're always in trees, they've learnt to eat, sleep and even give birth upside down.

3   The **pitcher plant**, found in South East Asian rainforests, is the largest meat-eating plant in the world. It's so big that it can even digest rats. But how? First, the plant attracts insects and small animals with a sweet-smelling sticky nectar. Second, the cup-shaped plant is an excellent trap. It's got slippery sides, so once the insects and other animals are inside, there's no escape! However, the pitcher plant doesn't 'eat' food the way animals do. First it needs to use chemicals to break down the protein and other nutrients in the meat, then it absorbs them.

4   The grass and plant-eating **hippopotamus** might be one of the deadliest creatures in Africa but it's got very sensitive skin, so living in the African heat is difficult. A hippo needs to spend most of its time in lakes or rivers. The water helps the hippo stay cool but it doesn't protect it from the sun's rays. Luckily, the hippo has adapted so that it can produce its own sunscreen!
Two acids in the hippo's skin combine to make a special gel which absorbs all the sun's harmful rays. It also stops skin infections when the hippo gets injured in fights.

5   So, next time you think that humans are the smartest creatures on the planet, think again! Humans might be intelligent but plants and animals can also do amazing things.

> **TIP**
> Knowing the meaning of word parts can help you work out the meaning of a word.
> **carni** = flesh
> **herbi** = herb or grass
> **vore** = swallow

15 Read the tip box next to the article. Are sloths, pitcher plants and hippopotami herbivores or carnivores? Why?

16 Look at 14. Read and answer.

1 Why do sloths burn energy slowly?

2 How much do sloths sleep?

3 Why do animals go to the pitcher plant?

4 Why can't insects that get into a pitcher plant climb out?

5 Why do hippos sit in water all day?

6 What is hippo sunscreen made of?

7 What else does hippo sunscreen do?

17 Look at 14. Read and complete in your notebook.

Sloth

Habitat: _rainforests in South and Central America_

Food: ¹

Interesting facts: .They move ². They eat and give birth ³.

Pitcher plant

Habitat: ⁴

Food: ⁵

Interesting facts: It's the largest ⁶. It produces a chemical which breaks down ⁷.

Hippopotamus

Habitat: ⁸

Food: ⁹

Interesting facts: It's one of ¹⁰. It has very ¹¹. It produces its own ¹².

18 Look at the animals in 13 or choose another amazing animal. Write an entry for an Amazing Animal fact file. Use the fact files in 17 to help you.

97

19 Listen and read. What are two important rules at Lakeside Camp?

FROM	Tom Spencer <t.spencer2003@my-mail.com>
SUBJECT	Lakeside Camp

Hi Sandy,
Camp started this week. Lakeside Camp is the best! We go swimming and canoeing every day and we sleep in wood cabins in the forest. I'm sharing with five other kids. Unfortunately, we have to tidy our cabin every day and we also have to take out the rubbish. There's a prize every day for the tidiest cabin. And no, we haven't won yet. :(
In the evenings, we can help with the cooking if we want but we don't have to. Usually we have barbecues. They're great because we use paper plates, so we don't have to do any washing-up!
I have to stop emailing now and get ready for my first windsurfing lesson. The teachers get cross if you're late for an activity. Two important rules at Lakeside Camp are: "You must be on time for activities" and "You mustn't be late for meals." Jim was late yesterday and now he has to pick up rubbish all day!
It's brilliant that you're coming to Lakeside next week! See you then.
Tom

20 Look at 19 and complete.

You **must/must not** do it: it's the rule.	You ¹ on time for activities. You ² late for meals.
You **have to** do it: it's necessary.	We ³ tidy our cabin. We ⁴ the rubbish. Jim ⁵ rubbish all day. What time **do** they **have to get up** at the camp?
You **don't have to do it**: it isn't necessary.	We **don't have to help** with the cooking. We ⁶ any washing-up. Tom **doesn't have to pick up** rubbish today.

Tip: Use **have to** in informal language and to talk about things that are necessary.
Use **must** to tell people what to do and to talk about formal rules.
Mustn't means "don't do it." **Don't have to** means "it isn't necessary."

21 Read and complete the rules at Lakeside Camp with must or mustn't.

1 You be on time for activities at the camp.

2 You play loud music after 9 p.m.

3 You ask a teacher if you want to use the computer room.

4 You turn your lights out at 10 p.m.

5 You go swimming in the lake on your own.

Read and complete the sentences with have/has to **or** don't/doesn't have to **and the verb.**

1 He 🔑 (take) a towel to go swimming. There are towels at the pool.

2 Mehmet took the rubbish out. We 🔑 (do) it.

3 Kate and Natalia 🔑 (get) good exam results so that they can go to university.

4 Larry didn't pass the test. He 🔑 (revise) and take it again.

5 Mark 🔑 (get) a visa so that he can travel to Spain.

6 I caught the school bus. Now I 🔑 (walk).

7 I 🔑 (buy) a better dictionary so that I can learn more English words.

 Choose the correct words.

1 We can sleep late tomorrow. We (mustn't/don't have to) get up early.

2 Hurry up! The play starts at two o'clock. We (mustn't/don't have to) be late.

3 The baby's sleeping. You (mustn't/don't have to) make too much noise.

4 Scott can use my sleeping bag. He (mustn't/doesn't have to) bring his.

5 I've got free tickets for the cinema. You (mustn't/don't have to) pay.

6 Shh! This is a Maths exam. You (mustn't/don't have to) talk.

 Complete the information about a summer school with have to, don't have to **or** mustn't.

1 Lessons start at 10:30 every day. Students 🔑 be late.

2 You 🔑 bring books or dictionaries. We'll give them to you.

3 There are optional fun activities at the end of each day. You 🔑 do them but we think you'll enjoy them.

4 You can bring your laptop but you 🔑 watch films or play games after 11 p.m.

5 All students 🔑 tidy their own rooms.

6 Students 🔑 use their mobile phones in class. If you want to make a call, please do it in the break.

25 **Think of six rules at your school. Write three rules with** must **and three rules with** mustn't **in your notebook.**

We must be on time for lessons.

We mustn't eat in the classroom.

Ancient Civilisations and Their Legacies

1   What do we take for granted in the world today – language, writing, theatre, politics? Even the subjects we learn about at school! In this article, we look at two civilisations which have had an important influence on the modern world.

2   The Greeks have had a great influence on modern culture. From 800 to 146 BC, the ancient Greeks shaped the world of art, literature and philosophy. Homer wrote his great works of literature in the 7th century BC, and Western philosophy was born with Socrates, Plato and Aristotle. The fascinating events and the myths and legends of ancient Greece have been a rich source of inspiration for films, plays and many famous works of art.

3   The ancient Greeks also gave the world a sporting legacy: the Olympic Games. The first games took place in the Greek city of Olympia in 776 BC. Today, as in ancient Greece, the modern Olympic Games still take place every four years.

26 Look at five ancient civilisations. When did they exist? Find them on the time line.

> the ancient Egyptians   the ancient Greeks   the Aztecs
> the Inca   the Maya

| 3150 BC | | | | 800 BC | | 146 BC | | | 900 AD | 1500 AD | |
| BC | | 2000 BC | | | 300 BC | | | | 1200 AD | | AD |

3150 BC–300 BC [1] 🐾   2000 BC–900 AD [2] 🐾

800 BC–146 BC [3] 🐾   1200 AD century–1500 AD [4] 🐾 and [5] 🐾

27 Look at the civilisations in 26 again. Which things below do you associate with them? Share your ideas with the class.

a Tutankhamen and the Pyramids   **b** the Olympic Games

c Machu Picchu   **d** organised agriculture

e chocolate   **f** Western philosophy

28 Read the article quickly and check your answers in 27. Which civilisation is not mentioned in the article?

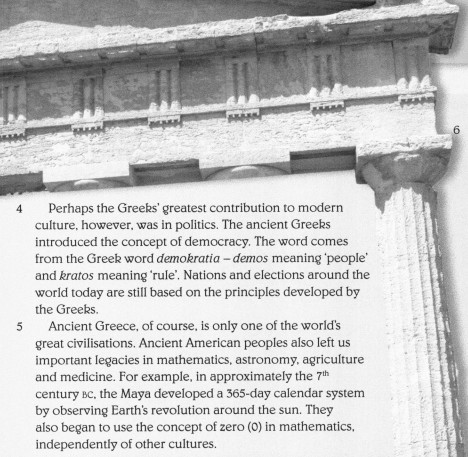

4   Perhaps the Greeks' greatest contribution to modern culture, however, was in politics. The ancient Greeks introduced the concept of democracy. The word comes from the Greek word *demokratia* – *demos* meaning 'people' and *kratos* meaning 'rule'. Nations and elections around the world today are still based on the principles developed by the Greeks.

5   Ancient Greece, of course, is only one of the world's great civilisations. Ancient American peoples also left us important legacies in mathematics, astronomy, agriculture and medicine. For example, in approximately the 7th century BC, the Maya developed a 365-day calendar system by observing Earth's revolution around the sun. They also began to use the concept of zero (0) in mathematics, independently of other cultures.

6   What about farming? If you enjoy chocolate, you can thank the people of the Aztec Empire, which was at its peak between the 14th and 16th centuries AD. The Aztecs were known for advancing the cultivation of cacao, a key ingredient in chocolate. The Inca civilisation, which was powerful in Peru when the Aztecs were powerful in Mexico, also introduced terraced farming, which is a special way of organising land for growing crops. This type of farming is still practised today. Many of the herbal remedies that we use to treat illnesses were also discovered by the Inca.

98

29   **Listen and read. Say** Greeks, Maya **or** Inca.

   1   They knew a lot about plant medicine.

   2   They developed an advanced political system.

   3   They developed a way of farming that's still used today.

   4   They used astronomy to measure time.

   5   They came from Peru.

   6   They produced great literary works.

30   **Research with a partner. In which centuries did the things below happen? Choose an event and find one or two more facts about it. Then tell the class.**

   1   The Declaration of Independence was signed, creating the United States of America.

   2   The first Olympic Games took place.

   3   King Khufu completed the Great Pyramid of Giza.

 THINK BIG **What else do you know about these ancient civilisations? Which other civilisations could you add to the time line?**

31 Read the fairy tale. Note down anything a character thinks, wonders, wishes or says.

The Ugly Duckling

A mother duck sat on her nest. One of her eggs was much larger than the others. She wondered why the egg was so big. Soon the egg hatched. Out came a very big and odd-looking duckling.

"PEEP!" said the big duckling and blinked.

"Go away!" the duckling's brother snapped. He told the duckling that he was the ugliest duckling he'd ever seen.

The poor duckling didn't know what to do so he ran away. Autumn came and went and soon winter chilled the air. The duckling shivered, cold and alone.

Finally, spring came and the duckling stretched his neck down to the water to drink. He saw a beautiful bird reflected in the water. He wished he could look like the bird in the reflection. "Then people wouldn't call me an ugly duckling," he said.

A little girl throwing bread to him heard what the duckling said. "But that *is* you!" she cried. "You're not an ugly duckling – you're a swan!"

32 Rewrite the story as a play. Complete it in your notebooks. Then read it aloud to a partner.

Narrator:	Mother Duck looks at her eggs.
Mother Duck: *[to herself]* ?	
Narrator:	The egg hatches. Out comes the Ugly Duckling.
Ugly Duckling: ?	
Ugly Duckling's brother: ?	
Narrator:	The Ugly Duckling runs away. Autumn and winter come and go. Spring arrives. The Ugly Duckling looks down at the water and sees something.
Ugly Duckling: *[to himself]* ?	
Little Girl: ?	

33 Work with a partner. Find a fairy tale. In your notebook, rewrite it as a play. Read your play aloud to the class.

34 The subjects you learn at school have practical and important uses in everyday life. Can you think of a practical use for each of your subjects? Copy and complete the chart.

School subject	Topic learnt	Everyday use
Literature	Myths and legends	help us recognise our faults; teach us valuable lessons about life and people
Maths		
Social Science		
Science		
Art and Music		
Health and P.E.		
English		

PROJECT

35 Work with a group. Make a book of names from ancient Greece that we use today.

1 Write the Greek name and say what it stood for.

2 Draw a picture.

3 Share your page. Explain why it's a good name to use today.

The Amazons were female Greek warriors. They were brave and strong. There's a company with this name that sells products online. The name makes people think that the company is strong.

Amazon

 THINK BIG Which is your least favourite school subject? Why? What can you do to learn to appreciate the knowledge it offers you?

36 107 Listen, read and repeat.

1 er **2** est

37 102 Listen and blend the sounds.

1 f-a-s-t-er   faster   **2** ea-s-i-er   easier

3 b-e-s-t   best   **4** ch-ea-p-er   cheaper

5 h-a-pp-i-er   happier   **6** l-o-n-g-e-s-t longest

38 103 Listen and chant.

Running is faster than walking,
Walking is cheaper than driving,
Driving is easier than flying,
Flying is harder than cycling,
Cycling is the best!

39 Make a sentence using the words in each row of the chart.

Pupil	Adjective	Activity
1 Hannah	most	has got books in her backpack
2 Robert	fewest	has got coins in his pockets
3 Cheryl	most	has got songs on her mp3 player
4 Dan	most	has got after-school activities every week
5 Paula	fewest	plays video games every day
6 Mark	least amount of	watches TV every day
7 Francis	most	watches films every month
8 Laura	least amount of	has got free time every week

40 Work with a partner. Ask and answer questions about the sentences you made in 39.

Who's got the most books in her backpack?

Hannah has.

41 Choose the correct form of the words in brackets. With a partner, research the answer to each question.

1 Which country has got (the most/more) pet dogs: Germany or the UK?

2 Which animal spends (the least/less) time eating: a cat or a panda?

3 What is (larger/the largest) mammal on the planet: the elephant or the blue whale?

4 Which country gives the (least/fewest) homework: China, the UK or Finland?

5 Which animal is (slower/the slowest): a snail, a sloth or a turtle?

6 Which place is the (fewest/least) populated place on Earth: the Galapagos Islands, Easter Islands or Antarctica?

7 Which is the (biggest/bigger) planet in the solar system: Mars or Jupiter?

8 Which planet has got the (fewest/least) moons: Venus, Earth or Mars?

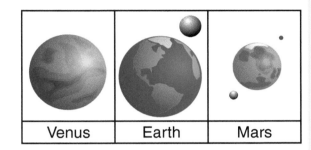

| Venus | Earth | Mars |

42 Complete the sentences with a word or phrase from the box.

> ancient democracy digest herbivore
> meat-eating playwright prime number sloth

1 Carnivores are ❓ plants or animals.

2 Shakespeare was a famous English ❓.

3 The Aztecs and the Maya were ❓ civilisations.

4 A ❓ is a slow animal that sleeps upside down.

5 A ❓ eats only plants and parts of plants.

6 A ❓ can be divided only by 1 and itself.

7 When you ❓ food, your body breaks it down.

8 A political system where the government is elected by the people is called a ❓.

I Can

- talk about school subjects and what I learn.
- identify some legacies of ancient civilisations.
- compare things using *more/most, fewer/fewest, less/least*.
- talk about rules and obligations.

How Well Do I Know It? Can I Use It?

1 Think about it. Read and draw. Practise.

🙂 I know this.   😐 I need more practice.   😟 I don't know this.

	PAGES			
Dreams: bring up a family, go on adventurous holidays, live in another country...	59	🙂	😐	😟
Super powers: read people's minds, become invisible...	75	🙂	😐	😟
School subjects: Music, English, Social Science...	90-91	🙂	😐	😟
Things we learn about: democracy, prime numbers...	90-91	🙂	😐	😟
What **will** you **be doing** ten years from now? I**'ll** definitely **be studying** at a big university in the city. I probably **won't be living** in Europe.	62-63	🙂	😐	😟
"I've got dreams. I'll travel the world." He **said that** he **had** dreams. He **said** he **would travel** the world.	66-67	🙂	😐	😟
If I **didn't have to go** to school, I**'d stay** at home all day. **If** you **could go** anywhere, where **would** you **go**? I**'d go** to Italy.	78-79	🙂	😐	😟
If I **won** a lot of money, I **might give** it to charity. **If** I **had** wings, I **could travel** for free!	82-83	🙂	😐	😟
China's got **more** speakers of English **than** the USA. I've got **fewer** school subjects **than** my brother. Some teachers give **less** homework **than** others.	94-95	🙂	😐	😟
The Amazon rainforest has got **the most** species of plants and animals on Earth. Cheltenham is one of **the least** populated cities in the UK. Antarctica's got **the fewest** flowering plants.	94-95	🙂	😐	😟
We **must be** on time. You **mustn't eat** in the classroom. I **have to help** my mum at home. We **don't have to get up** early tomorrow.	98-99	🙂	😐	😟

2 **Get ready.**

A   Number the lines of the dialogue in the correct order.
Then listen and check.

Calvin:	Yeah, maybe. But I'd like to try it and see. How about you? If you could have just one kind of food every day, what would it be?
Calvin:	Yes! I love pizza! I wish I could eat pizza every day.
Calvin:	What's for lunch tomorrow?
Calvin:	Yuck. If I only ate salad, I might get really thin! And I'd feel hungry all the time. It's too boring.
Calvin:	But I eat vegetables all the time… on pizza!
Hannah:	No, you don't. If you ate pizza every day, you'd get sick of it.
Hannah:	I asked Tom. He said it would be pizza again.
Hannah:	Well, it *wouldn't* be pizza. I think I'd have a salad every day.
Hannah:	Salad isn't boring, and you can't eat fat all the time. We have to eat some vegetables too!

B   Practise the dialogue in **A** with a partner.

C   Ask and answer the questions with a partner.

1   How does Calvin feel about tomorrow's lunch? How about Hannah?

2   Does Calvin like vegetables? Explain.

3   If you could choose one food to eat every day, what would it be? Why?

4   What do you think would happen if you ate that food every day?

Get set.

 STEP 1 Cut out the Mystery Classmate card on page 161 of your Activity Book.

STEP 2 Ask one classmate questions about him/her to fill in the card. Be sure to write neatly.

STEP 3 Mix up all the cards in a bag. Then each pupil takes one of the cards from the bag. Make sure it's not your own card. Now you're ready to **Go!**

Go!

A Work in a group. Take turns reading the information (except for the name) on your card aloud. Each group member copies the chart into a notebook and completes it by writing who he or she thinks the other group members are reading about.

Card number	Who read it?	Who do you think it's about?
Example	Andy	Anna
1	?	?
2	?	?
3	?	?
4	?	?

B Talk about your guesses. Give reasons for your choices.

I think Andy's card is about Anna. She loves playing football and she'll be working in a hospital someday.

I'm not sure. I don't think Anna likes chocolate.

C Each pupil says whose card he/she read in Step A. Check your guesses. Which person in your group solved the most mysteries?

5 **Write about yourself in your notebook.**

- If you could give any present to your best friend, what would it be? Why?
- If you could learn any skill instantly, what might you learn?
- What will you probably be doing twenty years from now?
- What are three important rules at your school?
- What are two things you have to do at home?

All About Me   Date:_____

_____

_____

How Well Do I Know It Now?

6 **Look at page 106 and your notebook. Draw again.**

A   Use a different colour.

B   Read and think.

I can start the next unit.

I can ask my teacher for help and then start the next unit.

I can practise and then start the next unit.

7 **Rate this Checkpoint.**

 very easy   easy   hard   very hard   fun   OK   not fun

Units 4-6 Exam Preparation

- Part A -

What dream does each pupil in Mr Brown's class have about the future?

 105

Listen and write a letter in each box. There is one example.

Vicky   B

Oliver   ☐

Susie   ☐

Adam   ☐

Kate   ☐

Justin   ☐

A   B   C   D

E   F   G   H

- Part B -

Read the letter and write the missing words. Write one word on each line.

Dear Robert,

Example   Last night, I _____***had***_____ the strangest dream. I dreamt

1   that I was a superhero with amazing powers! I _____

2   flying over cities and doing _____ of other things

3   and I felt very happy. The _____ interesting

part of my dream was when I travelled through time and

4   _____ back to the past. Of course, the people

back then didn't have the digital technology we've got today.

5   _____ I have the same dream again, I'd travel to the

future. That would be fun!

Maggie

MYSTERIES!

106

1 Can you identify these unsolved mysteries? Choose the name of the mystery from the box. Then listen carefully to check.

> Atlantis   Bermuda Triangle   crop circles   Kryptos   Nazca Lines

1 A prosperous city can't just disappear, can it? Plato, the Greek philosopher, wrote a detailed description of this island paradise. Today, there's no sign of it. Some say it was swallowed up by the sea – the result of an earthquake or a flood. What do you think? Did the island city Plato wrote about ever exist?

Mystery: 🔍

2 Most drawings don't have to be looked at from 305 metres above. But that's the only way you can see these 1,000-year old geoglyphs in Peru. Scientists don't know who made these enormous drawings of animals, plants and humans or why. It makes you wonder, doesn't it?

Mystery: 🔍

3 Here in this region of the Atlantic Ocean, compasses won't help you with directions. Ships and planes simply disappear here. What's causing this to happen? Is it pirates, methane gas in the water, human error or something else? No one knows. It's puzzling… and a little scary.

Mystery: 🔍

2 Look at the photos. What's the mystery all about? Read and match the mysteries to the descriptions. Then listen to check.

1

Crop circles

2

The Bermuda Triangle

3

The Great Pyramids

4

Northern lights

a How were these constructed in ancient times without the benefit of modern tools? It doesn't seem possible.

b Modern scientists have come up with a solid theory to explain these brilliant colours and have got proof to support their theory.

c These perfect geometrical patterns seem to appear overnight. There's no scientific explanation for this phenomenon.

d No one can explain why things disappear in this area. It's an unsolved mystery.

3 Work with a partner. Talk about the mysteries.

They don't know the answer to the crop circles mystery, do they?

No, they don't. There's no scientific explanation.

THINK BIG Choose one of the mysteries in 2, do some research to find out more about it and come up with your own explanation.

109

4

Listen and read. Where did the dry lake bed get its name from?

A MYSTERY? NOT ANY MORE!
The Sailing Stones (Death Valley, California)

Imagine this: Rocks of different sizes, some weighing more than 300 kilos, sit on a dried-up flat lake bed that goes on for kilometres and kilometres. You would think that these rocks, especially the heaviest and biggest ones, would just sit in one spot forever, wouldn't you? Not the ones in Death Valley, California, in the USA! You can see them on the enormous expanse of dry lake bed called Racetrack Playa, which is named after these 'racing' stones. Much to everyone's surprise, many of them, including the really big and heavy ones, have actually moved hundreds of metres from their original locations – but, of course, this happened when no one was looking.

Not only did the rocks and stones move far, some seemed to have stopped and changed direction! A few even turned around and moved back to their original locations! Rocks moving on their own isn't possible, is it? As you read this, you're probably thinking of all kinds of weird explanations. Before blaming this on extraterrestrial beings, read on.

In the 1970s, some long-term studies of the phenomenon were carried out. Scientists now believe this: every year, the dry lake bed gets flooded with melted snow from the surrounding mountains. The water softens the soil in the old lake bed, turning it into slippery mud. Although no one has actually seen the rocks move, the best guess is that wind then moves the rocks across the slippery surface of the lake bed. Sounds like a logical explanation, doesn't it? Indeed it is, but without anyone actually witnessing the phenomenon, doubters remain.

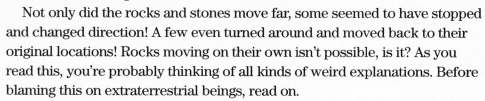
www.mysteryfans.com

Sebastian, Spain

Rocks that move? Pretty cool!

Emily, Australia

You don't really buy this whole story about stones moving, do you? Don't believe everything you read on the internet!

Liam, U.S.A.

Well, this story just happens to be true. I'm from California and the sailing stones have been studied since the 1940s. Even physicists have offered various theories. It's certainly not a hoax.

Georgina, UK

Wow, you're actually serious about these stones, aren't you? Do you guys believe that wind can actually make rocks move? Come on!

Detlef, Germany

I'm not totally convinced. There's got to be another explanation. Like pranksters, maybe?

Hiroto, Japan

I'm a geologist and rocks are my life. Believe me, Emily, these rocks really move! When the water level in the playa rises, the soil turns to mud and becomes slippery and strong winds cause the rocks to slide. Moderate winds can keep the rocks moving.

Liam, USA

Told you it's not a hoax. You're convinced now, aren't you?

READING COMPREHENSION

 Read and say true **or** false.

1 People have seen the rocks move 100 metres.
2 No one doubts the explanation given by scientists.
3 Their theory involves wind and water.
4 The rocks don't all move in the same direction.
5 The heaviest rocks don't move at all.

> **THINK BIG** Using objects or drawings, demonstrate and describe the various movements of the rocks in Racetrack Playa. Do you think pranksters are responsible for moving the rocks? Do you agree with scientists' explanation for the rocks moving? Why/Why not?

6 Listen and read. What's the big mystery?

James: Hey, Kyle. Have you heard about Kryptos?

Kyle: Ummm. I think so.

James: You haven't got a clue, have you?

Kyle: Yeah, I have. It's a video game, isn't it?

James: Nope – not even close. It's a sculpture.

Kyle: A sculpture of what?

James: Let me see if I can find a picture... Yep, here's one.

Kyle: Hmm, it's just letters of the alphabet. So why would anyone have a sculpture like that?

James: The letters are really four encrypted messages. You need to work out the code to read the secret messages.

Kyle: But nobody can read the messages, can they?

James: Of course not! I think the idea is to challenge code breakers.

Kyle: You're probably right. Has anyone decoded them yet?

James: Yes, three have been decoded. But the fourth one is still a mystery.

7 Practise the dialogue in 6 with a partner.

8 Listen and match. Then choose the correct ending to the question.

1 Ancient people made these, (did they/didn't they)?

2 These are very beautiful, (are they/aren't they)?

3 People can't break the code, (can they/can't they)?

4 This place hasn't been found, (has it/hasn't it)?

AFFIRMATIVE STATEMENTS	NEGATIVE TAGS	NEGATIVE STATEMENTS	POSITIVE TAGS
The geoglyphs **are** in Peru, Experts **have** explained them, We **solved** the mystery,	**aren't** they? **haven't** they? **didn't** we?	Atlantis **isn't** real, Scientists **haven't** found it, It **didn't** make sense,	**is** it? **have** they? **did** it?

Tip: Use question tags with falling intonation when you expect someone to agree with you.

9 Choose the correct question tags in brackets.

1 The northern lights are a natural phenomenon, (are they/aren't they)?

2 They are also called the aurora borealis, (are they/aren't they)?

3 The aurora borealis isn't a comet, (is it/isn't it)?

4 People in ancient times knew about the northern lights, (did they/didn't they)?

5 They're not visible in Asia, (are they/aren't they)?

6 Scientists haven't explained the aurora borealis yet, (have they/haven't they)?

10 Prepare to interview an archaeologist about Atlantis. Make question tags.

1. A: In your article, you claimed that Atlantis existed, ❓
   B: Yes, I did...

2. A: You don't know the exact location of the city, ❓
   B: No, I don't...

3. A: Your article claims that you have found artefacts, ❓
   B: Yes, it does...

4. A: Most scientists disagree with your research, ❓
   B: Yes, they do, but...

11 Write responses for the archaeologist in the interview in 10. Then role play the interview with a partner.

12 Work with a partner. Guess and complete the messages with words in the box.

> coloured lights northern lights North Pole winter

Aurora borealis is a display of ¹ ? , isn't it?

You can see it better from the ³ ? , can't you?

I think so. And it's also called ² ? .

Yes, I think so. I know that it's more visible in ⁴ ? .

115

13 Listen and read. Check your answers in 12.

> **CONTENT WORDS**
> altitude atmosphere clapping interaction nitrogen observe
> oxygen phenomenon pole solar wind stand out swirling

The Aurora Borealis

1. Albert Einstein, whose work we still study today, once said this about nature: "What I see in nature is a magnificent structure that we can comprehend only very imperfectly and that must fill a thinking person with a feeling of humility." We could surely say this while looking at the aurora borealis!

2. The aurora borealis, also called the northern lights, is a magnificent display of swirling coloured lights that's visible in northern countries. Each year people even travel closer to the North Pole to see it and enjoy its beauty. While modern films are full of special effects, this is a natural effect that's truly amazing.

3. What causes this strange phenomenon? For a long time, no one could answer this question. People thought it was just a mysterious natural event or even the spirits of animals they had hunted. Recently however, science has provided an explanation – the lights are caused by the interaction of solar winds with oxygen and nitrogen in the upper part of the Earth's atmosphere. The solar winds, which come from the sun, are attracted to the Earth's poles – the Arctic and the Antarctic, which is why auroras are easier to see at these places. The different colours of an aurora mean that solar winds are interacting with different gases at different altitudes. Oxygen produces yellow-green and red colours and nitrogen produces violets and blues.

4. The northern lights are easiest to see in the Arctic from autumn to early spring. This is the time of year when nights are long and dark and the colours really stand out. However, during strong solar storms, you can sometimes see the aurora borealis as far south as Texas. At the South Pole, a similar phenomenon occurs at the same time as the one in the north. This is called the aurora australis, or southern lights. Scientists have also observed aurora displays on Jupiter, Saturn, Uranus, Neptune and Mars.

5. Scientists have discovered a lot about the aurora borealis but some things are still a mystery. For example, people have said that a clapping sound comes at the same time as the light display. Whatever the explanation, the aurora's magical and mysterious beauty has inspired and continues to inspire painters, poets and songwriters.

14 **Look at** 13. **Read and say** true **or** false.

1 Albert Einstein discovered the aurora borealis.

2 Scientists explained the aurora borealis a long time ago.

3 The colours of the aurora borealis are created when gases react with solar winds.

4 The aurora has got different colours because of reactions with different gases.

5 The aurora borealis is easiest to see when the sky is dark.

6 You can see the aurora australis at different times of the year to the borealis.

15 **Use the text to complete the facts about the aurora borealis.**

- You might see the aurora borealis in Texas during [1] .
- The northern lights have inspired [2] .
- Some people believed the aurora borealis was the spirits [3] .
- The beautiful colours in the aurora include [4] .

16 **Work in groups. Look at some notes about another interesting natural phenomenon. Put the notes together to make a paragraph. Write in your notebook.**

ice circles
caused by ice rotating in water
different sizes; biggest are more than 15 m wide
occur in cold water and climates
reported sightings in Scandinavia and North America

THINK BIG Does nature make you feel humble? Which things in nature do you think are really beautiful?

17 Listen and read. What time are Joe and Suzy going to get up tomorrow? Where are they going to have breakfast?

Joe: I woke up really late this morning.

Suzy: So did I! I didn't wake up until eleven and I still feel half-asleep.

Joe: I'm going to try and get up earlier tomorrow.

Suzy: OK. So am I. I don't want to sleep all morning again.

Joe: Neither do I. I know, let's get up at eight and go to the pool until ten.

Suzy: Yeah, for a two-hour swim!

Joe: We could have a picnic in the park after that.

Suzy: Wow! A picnic breakfast? I haven't done that before.

Joe: Neither have I, but it's good to try new things, isn't it?

Suzy: I suppose so. But you know, last time I got up early, I was tired and bad-tempered all day.

Joe: So was I! Let's get up at nine thirty!

18 Copy the information. Look at 17 again and complete.

> **Compound adjectives** have two or more words.
>
> **half-** ¹?, a ²?**-tempered** child, a ³? swim, a **five-euro** note, a **twelve-year-old** boy

19 Complete the compound adjectives with the words.

> awake   fashioned   kilometre   known   looking   sleeved

1 My grandma is really old-?. She never uses email!

2 I went to bed at two in the morning, so I'm only half-? today.

3 It's really hot today. Where's my short-? shirt?

4 Lucas is tall and good-?, like a film star.

5 We went for a three-? run in the park. We're exhausted!

6 She isn't a world famous pop star but she's quite a well-? musician.

20 Look at 17 again and complete.

SHORT AGREEMENTS: POSITIVE	SHORT AGREEMENTS: NEGATIVE
A: I **woke** up late. **B: So** [1] ❓ I!	**A:** I **don't** want to sleep all morning. **B: Neither** [4] ❓ I!
A: I **was** bad-tempered all day. **B: So** [2] ❓ I!	
A: I**'m** going to get up earlier. **B:** [3] ❓ I!	**A:** I **haven't** done that before. **B:** [5] ❓ I!
Tip: Never makes a sentence negative. I**'ve never** done it. **Neither** have I.	

21 Choose the correct agreement.

1 **A:** I don't wake up without an alarm.   **B:** (So do I./Neither do I.)

2 **A:** Fatih isn't coming on the trip.   **B:** (Neither isn't Ben./Neither is Ben.)

3 **A:** Katie can stand on her head.   **B:** (Neither can I./So can Hande.)

4 **A:** I've never seen that film.   **B:** (So has Andy./Neither has Andy.)

5 **A:** My parents were annoyed with me.   **B:** (So were mine./So did mine.)

22 Complete the short agreements. Follow the example.

1 **A:** I don't believe in ghosts.   **B:** _Neither do_ I.

2 **A:** I've never seen the northern lights.   **B:** ❓ I.

3 **A:** My sister is really interested in unsolved mysteries.   **B:** ❓ mine.

4 **A:** I think crop circles are a hoax.   **B:** ❓ my friend Dan.

5 **A:** I won't ever fly over the Bermuda Triangle.   **B:** ❓ I.

6 **A:** We aren't convinced that rocks can move.   **B:** ❓ we.

23 Take turns asking and answering questions. Then agree or disagree and add some information. Use these ideas.

> Are you good at … ?   Are you sometimes … ?   Can you … ?
> Did you …yesterday/on Saturday ?   Do you hate … ?
> Do you like … ?   Have you been to … ?

Can you dance the tango?

No, I can't.

Neither can I. It's really difficult.

Mysterious Findings

1   There are stories of strange discoveries, unexplained artefacts and mysterious sightings from all over the world. These phenomena become part of a country's culture. Studying them is popular with curious people and with scientists who want to find explanations. However, some things, such as how people built the Pyramids, or what happens in the Bermuda Triangle, simply can't be explained. Here are two interesting examples from Costa Rica and Tibet.

Stone Spheres

2   Take a look at this photograph. These stones don't look natural, do they? In 1930, while clearing an area of the Costa Rican jungle, workers came upon a number of these balls, which are estimated to date back to 600 BC. Since then, several hundred have been discovered and they're all perfectly constructed! They vary in size from the size of tennis balls to spheres that are 2.4 metres in diameter and weigh 16 tons.

24   **Look at the questions. Answer with a partner, then share your ideas with the class.**

1   When people visit your country, what do they come to see?

2   Are there any unusual myths, legends, monuments or places in your country?

3   Are there any explanations for these strange things?

25   **Read the article quickly and find these words and numbers. Then make quick sentences with the phrases in the box.**

1   jungle

2   16

3   1930

4   600

5   a gorilla

6   Sasquatch

> another name for
> discovered in
> looks like
> made in
> weigh

3 Studies have shown that the balls are made of granodiorite, a rock which is easy to break when its temperature changes rapidly from hot to cold. Researchers believe that ancient civilisations made the balls using hot coals and cold water. First, they broke the rock so that the balls were almost spherical. Then they used ancient tools to make the rock smooth. However, even with today's technology, getting the stones this perfect would be extremely difficult. The mystery remains: who made the stones and why? And how did they give them such a perfect shape?

The Yeti

4 You've heard of the yeti, haven't you? So have I. But like most people, I wonder if it's real or just a legend. People believe that the yeti, also called the abominable snowman, resembles a gorilla. Many believe that the yeti lives in the Himalayan regions of Tibet and Nepal, which is where the legend began. But people also talk about a yeti-like creature in Canada and Alaska, where he's called Sasquatch.

5 Over the years, scientists and explorers have tried to find evidence for the existence of the yeti. So far, only footprints have been found. There's no proof that a yeti or any other creature made them and photographs are never clear. Many scientists think that they were probably made by bears. So why do people continue to believe the yeti exists? Maybe because there's no proof that it doesn't exist... and because people like mysteries!

118

26 Listen and read. Choose the best answer.

1 Who discovered the stone spheres?
   a Scientists in the jungle.
   b Tourists visiting an important site.
   c Workers clearing trees.

2 The spheres are all...
   a the same size.
   b different shapes and sizes.
   c perfectly round.

3 Granodiorite is...
   a a kind of rock.
   b difficult to break and shape.
   c man-made.

4 Which statement is true?
   a Nobody has seen the yeti.
   b There's proof that the yeti exists.
   c The yeti is also called the abominable snowman.

5 The legend of the yeti comes from...
   a the people of the Himalayas.
   b literature.
   c Canada and Alaska.

27 Look at 26. What explanations are there in the article for the mysteries? Can you think of any more? Collect ideas with your class.

28 Read this explanation for why the Sailing Stones move.

What Causes the Sailing Stones to Move

The Racetrack Playa in Death Valley gets seven to ten centimetres of rain a year but the rainfall comes in bursts. During the storms, the ground floods and the fine soil turns into mud and becomes very slippery. The winds, which can reach 145 kilometres per hour, can actually overcome the force of friction and cause the stones to move. Once the stones are already moving, much less powerful winds can keep them in motion.

29 Now copy and complete the missing words in the chart.

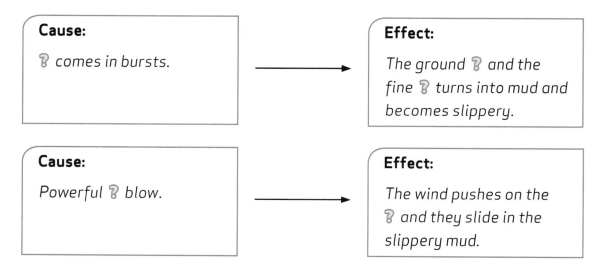

Cause:

❓ comes in bursts.

→

Effect:

The ground ❓ and the fine ❓ turns into mud and becomes slippery.

Cause:

Powerful ❓ blow.

→

Effect:

The wind pushes on the ❓ and they slide in the slippery mud.

 30 In your notebook, write your own cause-and-effect paragraph. Choose a topic from your personal experience or from your Science or Social Science class. Before you write, make a chart like the one in 29. Use your chart to write the paragraph. Share your paragraph with the class.

> **THINK BIG** What do you think are the advantages of being curious and asking lots of questions? Are there any disadvantages?

31 Is curiosity important? Say which statements you agree with. Then discuss your opinions with a partner.

1 Curiosity makes us ask questions and questions help us learn.

2 Curiosity makes us unhappy and dissatisfied.

3 Curiosity leads to answers or solutions.

4 Curiosity encourages us to be creative.

5 Curiosity leads to inventions and discoveries.

6 Curiosity makes us look indecisive, like we don't know something.

32 Curious minds solve mysteries. How curious are you? Keep a curiosity diary for a week.

1 Copy these suggestions into your notebook:

Ask questions. / Be observant. / Find answers. / Study one new topic every day. / Try something new. / Read a lot!

2 Write in your diary every day. Give details that show your curiosity.

3 When your diary is complete, discuss it with a partner.

Monday, 17ᵗʰ March

I was observant. I looked at a frog under a magnifying glass.

PROJECT

At Ringing Rocks Park in Pennsylvania, USA, when you hit the rocks with a hammer, they sound like bells. That's unusual, isn't it? But it's true. And no one knows why it happens.

33 Did the things you read in this unit make you curious? Learn more about mysterious earth or science phenomena.

A Make a booklet with a partner. Research information about two mysteries. Use these headers for each topic:

• General Information
• Research Done
• Theories Found
• My Conclusion

B When you have finished, share your booklet with another pair.

Mystery #1:
Ringing Rocks Park,
Pennsylvania, USA

<u>General Information</u>
The rocks sound like bells when you hit them.

<u>Research Done</u>
http://www.travelandleisure.com/travel-guide/bucks-county/activities/ringing-rocks-park

<u>Theories Found</u>
There are no explanations for this phenomenon.

<u>My Conclusion</u>
I think they must be made of something unusual.

120

34 Listen, read and repeat.

1 un **2** inter **3** re **4** pre **5** super

121

35 Listen and blend the sounds.

1 un-h-a-pp-y   unhappy   **2** inter-n-a-t-io-n-a-l   international

3 re-c-y-c-le   recycle   **4** pre-u-s-ed   preused

5 Super-m-a-n   Superman   **6** re-d-u-ce   reduce

122

36 Listen and chant.

> Celebrate International Earth Day!
> Recycle your Superman T-shirt
> And your pre-washed bottles.
> Reduce unhealthy food,
> Try healthy food! It's good!

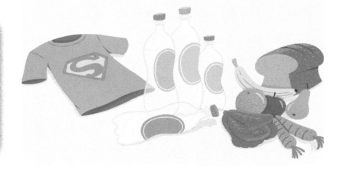

37 Work in a small group. Do a survey. Which mystery is your favourite? Make a graph to show what your classmates' favourite mystery is.

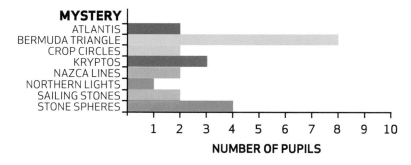

38 Ask and answer questions about the results. Use question tags when you can.

The Bermuda Triangle is our favourite mystery, isn't it?

I think it's because it's still unsolved.

Yeah. I wonder why.

Maybe but I think it's because it's creepy.

39 Complete the sentences using question tags. Then give answers to show you agree or disagree.

> I think so. We can't solve them unless we investigate them.

1 All unsolved mysteries are worth investigating, ?
2 Some mysteries can't be solved even with scientific research, ?
3 Curiosity makes new discoveries and inventions possible, ?
4 Einstein had a curious mind, ?
5 You haven't heard of the Ringing Rocks, ?

40 Read and complete with words from the box. Then complete the agreements.

> five-year-old   ten-pound   old-fashioned   400-metre

1 **A:** I bought a ? dress.
  B: So ?.

2 **A:** I've got a ? brother.
  B: ?

3 **A:** I don't like ? houses.
  B: Neither ?.

4 **A:** I won't run in the ? race.
  B: ?

41 Complete the sentences with words from the box.

> phenomenon   proof   scientific   theory   unsolved

1 So far, there is no ? explanation for how the stones became so perfectly round.
2 One ? that explains the mystery of Atlantis is that it disappeared during a large earthquake.
3 Actually, there's no reliable ? that the city of Atlantis ever existed.
4 The aurora borealis is a natural ? that has been explained.
5 The mystery of the stone spheres is still ?.

I Can

- **discuss mysterious phenomena.**
- **confirm information using question tags.**
- **agree using So/Neither.**
- **use compound adjectives.**

unit 8 WHY IS IT FAMOUS?

1 Work with a partner. Look at the map and the pictures of the places. Match the places to the names in the box. Then listen to check.

1

2

3

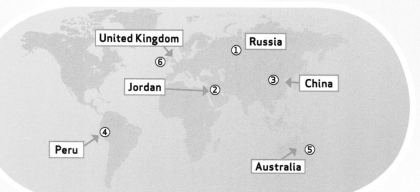

United Kingdom
⑥
Russia ①
Jordan → ②
③ ← China
Peru → ④
⑤
Australia

City of Petra
Forbidden City
Machu Picchu
St Basil's Cathedral
Stonehenge
Sydney Opera House

4

5

6

2 Share your results with the class. Who identified the most places correctly?

3 Discuss in small groups.
- Have you ever heard about any of these places? Which ones?
- Why are they famous?

4 Look at the photos and read the information about each. Then listen and complete.

**1 Big Ben
(the Elizabeth Tower)**

Location:
London, UK
When it was completed: [?]

2 Taj Mahal

Location:
Agra, [?]
When it was built:
between 1632–1654

3 Temple of Borobudur

Location:
Central Java, Indonesia
When it was built:
in the [?] and [?] centuries

4 Great Sphinx of Giza

Location:
Giza, [?]
When it was built:
probably between
2558–2532 BC

5 Statue of Liberty

Location:
New York City Harbour, USA
When it was dedicated: [?]

**6 Pyramid of Kukulcán
(El Castillo) at
Chichén Itzá**

Location:
Yucatan Peninsula, Mexico
When it was built:
around [?] AD

5 Look at 4. Listen and match the descriptions to the places. Note down any new information you learn.

6 Work with a partner. Talk about the famous places and things. Give as much information as you can.

Is Big Ben a clock, a tower or a bell?

It's a bell. It hangs inside the Elizabeth Tower in London.

THINK BIG Choose a famous landmark in your country, research the facts you don't know about it and present it to the class.

Listen and read. What is another name for Easter Island?

The Mysteries of Easter Island

For hundreds of years, Easter Island has been a place shrouded in mystery. Have the mysteries of this faraway island finally been solved?

Full of mysteries, Easter Island is a small island that sits in the Pacific Ocean, about 3,500 kilometres to the west of Chile, South America. It is a volcanic island that may once have had a population of 7,000–17,000 people. Today, there are only 4,000 people who live on the island.

Easter Island, known as Rapa Nui to the original settlers, was discovered by Dutch explorers on Easter Day in 1722. Most people know Easter Island today because of the giant statues there, called *moai*.

For a long time, no one was sure about where the people of Rapa Nui were from. Thanks to DNA testing of old bones, we now know that the original people of Rapa Nui were from Polynesia.

For many years, the statues were also the subject of mystery.

For many years, the statues were also the subject of mystery. The faces of the statues looked expressionless. Many scientists thought the statues represented dead ancestors. In 1979, scientist Sergio Rapu Haoa discovered that long ago the statues had eyes that were made of coral. Since his discovery, many of the eyes of the moai have been restored. With eyes, the statues' faces look very different. They look like proud, strong leaders who watch over Rapa Nui.

Moai on Easter Island

Probably the biggest mystery about the statues today is still this: how were these statues – most of which are over 4 metres tall and weigh more than 12 tons – moved from the quarry where they were carved out of volcanic rock to various locations around the island?

Some scientists believe the Rapa Nui people used trees to move the statues. They think the tree trunks were used as rollers, or sleds, to pull the statues across the island. Other scientists, however, believe the statues were 'walked' across the island. They think ropes were used to rock the statues from side to side, moving them forward a little each time they were rocked. And some people even believe that the statues were moved by aliens with sophisticated technology who helped the Rapa Nui people put the statues in new locations.

Scientists have discovered a lot about this ancient culture over just the last fifty years. Maybe someday they will solve all of its mysteries.

Moai with eyes restored

READING COMPREHENSION

8 **Read and say** true **or** false. **Compare your answers with a partner.**

1 The population of Easter Island today is about 7,000.

2 Easter Island is famous because it was discovered on Easter Day.

3 DNA of old bones was used to find out where the people of Rapa Nui were from.

4 In 1979, a scientist discovered that the moai once had eyes that were made of coral.

5 One unsolved mystery is how the statues were moved to different locations on the island.

How do you think the moai were moved to their locations around the island? Explain.
What other places do you know of that hold mysteries like this?

129

9 Listen and read. What places can Juan and his family visit without going very far?

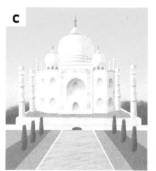

Juan: Do you know what Mum told me? We don't appreciate things that are close to us – right here in Taos.

Dad: She's right. This town's got a lot of history.

Juan: Remember the family who was visiting from London last summer?

Dad: I do. They were really excited about seeing the old churches here.

Juan: Yeah, and we had never been to *any* that were on their list! They were really surprised, weren't they?

Dad: Yeah. But thanks to that family, we finally got to see the inside of the Church of San Francisco de Asís.

Juan: The one that was rebuilt? That was cool. You know, Dad, maybe we should visit more of the famous places that are around us. How about the Taos Ski Valley? It's known all over the world!

Dad: I *knew* you had a reason for bringing this up. You want to go on a ski trip!

10 Practise the dialogue in 9 with a partner.

130

11 Listen and match. Then complete the sentences with the correct form of a verb from the box.

build   bury
design   take

a    **b**    **c**   **d**

1 It ? on an island.   **2** The photographs ? in Mexico.   **3** The emperor's wife ? in this place.   **4** It ? by an architect from Denmark.

Active	Passive
Archaeologists discovered Machu Picchu in 1911.	Machu Picchu **was discovered** in 1911 (by archaeologists).

12 **Say whether each sentence is** active **or** passive.

1 The Taj Mahal is visited by millions of tourists each year.

2 Alexandre Gustave Eiffel designed Paris's Eiffel Tower.

3 Two hundred thousand workers constructed the Forbidden City.

4 Petra, Jordan, was made a new wonder of the world by millions of voters.

5 The Sydney Opera House was opened to the public in 1973.

Leonardo da Vinci is the famous artist and inventor **who painted** the Mona Lisa. The Eiffel Tower is a landmark **that has become** the symbol of Paris, France.

Tip: A relative clause describes a noun. The relative pronouns *who* and *that* are used to describe people; *that* is used to describe things.

13 **Rewrite the two sentences as one sentence in your notebook.**

1 The Statue of Liberty is a landmark. It has become a symbol of welcome.

2 Van Gogh was a famous Dutch painter. He painted *Starry Night*.

3 The Leaning Tower of Pisa is a famous landmark. It leans to one side.

4 The Taj Mahal is a beautiful mausoleum. It was built in memory of Mumtaz Mahal.

5 Michelangelo was a famous artist. He painted the ceiling of the Sistine Chapel.

6 King Tutankhamen was a young king. He ruled Egypt during the 18th dynasty.

7 The Burj Al Arab is a luxurious hotel. It's located in Dubai.

8 Santiago Calatrava is a Spanish architect. He designed the Turning Torso, the tallest building in Sweden.

9 The Alhambra is a palace in Andalusia, Spain. It was originally constructed as a fortress.

10 The Great Wall of China is a type of fortification. It is 21,196 kilometres long.

14 Read and answer with a partner. Check your answers with the class.

1 What's an archaeologist?

2 What's an archaeological site?

3 Are there any archaeological sites near you? What do you know about them?

15 Listen and read. Which archaeologist discovered the tomb of King Tutankhamen?

CONTENT WORDS

archaeologist artefact carving dig excavate goddess
mummified pharaoh remains tomb treasure

Accidental Discoveries

1 Finding things from the past is exciting. Archaeologists spend years studying ancient texts and history books in order to discover ancient places. Tombs, palaces, important treasures, sometimes whole cities are hidden underground under layers of earth and rock. Sometimes they're found after careful research and digging but sometimes they're discovered by accident! Here are two truly amazing accidental discoveries.

2 In 1978, a new subway system for Mexico City was being constructed near the national cathedral. As the workers were digging, they discovered a huge carved stone! The stone was over three metres round and about 30 centimetres thick. It weighed just over 8.5 tons. Workers had archaeologists brought in. They immediately confirmed that the stone was a giant carving of the Aztec moon goddess.

3 The archaeologists quickly realized that this was an important discovery. These were the remains of an Aztec temple from the ancient city of Tenochtitlan. Soon a pyramid was uncovered, which scientists dated to 1325 AD! Built on top of the original pyramid there were another six pyramids. In total, over 7,000 different artefacts were also found at the site. Before this surprise discovery, archaeologists believed that Spanish people had destroyed the temple to build the cathedral. Today, if you visit the Zócalo, which is in the heart of Mexico City, you can see the artefacts in the Templo Mayor Museum nearby.

4 The discovery of King Tutankhamen's tomb in the Valley of the Kings in Egypt might be the most famous accidental discovery of its kind. The Valley is home to more than 60 tombs in which ancient pharaohs and kings are buried. In 1922, most archaeologists had given up looking for tombs there because they were convinced that everything had already been discovered. But one archaeologist, Howard Carter, continued searching.

5 Carter decided to excavate under the remains of some abandoned huts from an old archaeological dig. He was not disappointed. Working with some friends of his, he discovered the entrance to the tomb of King Tutankhamen. The tomb, containing the mummified body of the pharaoh, a gold coffin and more than 2,000 magnificent treasures, is the most well-preserved ancient tomb that has ever been found. The tomb survived 3,000 years, even though robbers and floods destroyed many of the other tombs in the region. The artefacts from the tomb that once belonged to King Tutankhamen can now be seen in the Cairo Museum in Egypt.

16 Read the article quickly and complete.

Name of site	Aztec temple of Tenochtitlan	Tomb of King Tutankhamen
Location	¹ ?	Valley of the Kings, Egypt
Dates back to	1325 AD	² ?
Discovered in	³ ?	1922
Discovered by	Workers digging	⁴ ?
Artefacts found	⁵ ?	⁶ ?
Where can you see them?	Templo Mayor Museum, Mexico City	⁷ ?

17 Look at 15. Read and say Mexico City or Egypt.

1 archaeologists believed it had been destroyed
2 were destroyed by thieves and water
3 six other similar constructions
4 people thought there was nothing interesting to find
5 a very rich archaeological site
6 in the busy city centre

18 Work with a partner. Look at some information about two more ancient sites. Then ask and answer with the prompts.

Tomb of Qin Shi Huang
China, 246–208 BC
In 1974, workers digging a well
Thousands of clay soldiers, some riding horse or chariots, some with paint on

Unesco site of Hagar Qim
Malta, 2400–200 BC
In 1839, engineers discovered it under rocks
Several ancient temples with carvings, stone statues

What/name?   How old/it?   Where/found?
Who/discover it?   What artefacts/found there?

Grammar

19 Listen and read. What's the problem with Olly's bike? Is he going to mend it himself?

Emma: What happened to your bike? Why's the wheel all bent?

Olly: I left it on a street corner last night and a car must have hit it.

Emma: That's really annoying. People shouldn't drive so fast.

Olly: I know. Now I need to get it repaired.

Emma: You need to have the wheel replaced.

Olly: How much do you think that will be? Have you ever had that done?

Emma: Yes. I had a wheel replaced on my bike last year and it cost €180.

Olly: That's really expensive! Do you think I could mend it myself?

Emma: I suppose so… but it could be quite tricky.

Olly: You're right. I'll get it fixed at the bike shop.

20 Look at 19 and complete.

have/get something done
Now I need to ¹ 🔲 . (ask someone to repair it for me)
You need to ² 🔲 . (someone needs to replace the wheel for you)
I ³ 🔲 on my bike last year.
I think I'll ⁴ 🔲 at the bike shop.
Have you ever ⁵ 🔲 ? (Has anyone ever done that for you?)

21 Read and make sentences with the words.

1 her hair / had / My friend / dyed blonde / last week.
   My friend had her hair dyed blonde last week.

2 When / getting / are they / cleaned? / their car

3 clothes / made for you? / Have you ever / had

4 have / repaired. / my watch / I need to

5 Where / get / going to / are you / painted? / your nails

6 needs to / Mum / get / done. / her hair

22 Read and complete. Use the words in brackets.

1 **A:** Has Sarah had her eyes tested yet?

   B: No, _she's having them tested_ tomorrow. (having/tested)

2 **A:** Did Belma get her laptop mended yesterday?

   B: Yes, at the new computer shop. (got/mended)

3 **A:** How often do you usually have your hair cut?

   B: every six months. (have/cut)

4 **A:** Has Adnan ever had his photo taken by a professional?

   B: Yes, last week – for his passport. (had/taken)

23 Match the problems to the things you need to have done.

1 glasses broken   **a** clean it

2 coat dirty   **b** cut it

3 hair too long   **c** mend them

4 jeans too long   **d** test them

5 leg broken   **e** paint them

6 eyes giving me problems   **f** shorten them

7 walls a bit dirty   **g** x-ray it

24 Look at 23. **Make sentences with** haven't had … yet **and** going to get … soon. **Follow the example.**

1 My glasses are broken. I haven't had them mended
   yet but I'm going to get them mended soon.

25 Make true sentences about you, your family or friends, using get/have something done. **Use these phrases or your own ideas. Share with the class.**

> a tooth filled   clothes made   ears pierced
> eyes tested   house painted   photo taken

My friend had her eyes tested last week.   **I'm getting my ears pierced next year!**

The New Seven World Wonders

What exactly are the Seven Wonders of the World? Who created the list and when?

1 The list has existed since antiquity. It's a list of the most amazing natural and man-made structures on earth. The list was first compiled by the historian Herodotus in the 5th century BC. His list was created using sights which were popular with Hellenic sightseers. The original list therefore included sites from the Mediterranean only. The number seven was chosen because the Greeks believed seven was a perfect number. Only one of the original ancient wonders still exists today – the Great Pyramid of Giza in Egypt.

2 Over the years there have been a number of different lists, but in 2001, a Swiss company decided to have a new list made, with seven wonders of the modern world. They chose 21 finalists. Of course, the Great Pyramid of Giza was added to the list and became the honorary eighth wonder.

26 Look at some famous places and attractions around the world. Where are they? What do you know about them? Collect information with your class.

> the Amazon River   the Eiffel Tower   the Galapagos Islands
> the Great Pyramids   the Statue of Liberty   the Taj Mahal

27 Look at the article quickly. Which is the oldest wonder of the modern world?

28 Copy the chart. Where are the seven wonders of the modern world? Read the article quickly and complete.

Asia	Taj Mahal
Europe	
The Americas	

These are the places that received the final vote:

3 **1 Petra:** Possibly built as early as the 6ᵗʰ century BC, this was the capital of an ancient empire. The structures of this city in Jordan, Western Asia were carved into rock and sandstone.

2 Taj Mahal: When Mumtaz Mahal, the wife of Emperor Shah Jahan, died, the Indian Emperor had this temple built – between 1632 and 1654.

3 Great Wall of China: Built between the 5ᵗʰ century BC and the 16ᵗʰ century AD. This wall was built more than 2,000 years ago to keep enemies out.

4 Kukulcán Pyramid at Chichén Itzá: Built sometime between the 11ᵗʰ and 13ᵗʰ centuries AD, Chichén Itzá is an archaeological site on the Yucatan Peninsula. Kukulcán, a 30-metre-high pyramid and temple, is its most famous landmark.

5 Machu Picchu: Built in the early 15ᵗʰ century AD. This ancient Incan city is 2,430 metres above sea level and consists of 150 buildings. Its most famous structure, the Temple of the Sun, is made of solid rock.

6 Statue of Christ the Redeemer: Built between 1922 and 1931. Standing 38 metres tall at the top of a mountain is a statue of Christ with his arms outstretched. The statue looks out over the city of Rio de Janeiro, Brazil.

7 Roman Colosseum: Built between 72 and 80 AD. During the Roman Empire, the Colosseum was used for battles between gladiators and for other forms of entertainment.

Which other place would get your vote as the eighth wonder?

136

29 Listen and read. Then answer the questions.

1 Who created the first list of wonders?

2 Why were there seven?

3 When was the modern list created?

4 What was Petra made of?

5 Why was the Great Wall of China built?

6 Who was Mumtaz Mahal?

7 What's Kukulcán?

8 Which wonder was built after 1900?

30 Work with a partner. Design a structure that could be a wonder in your country. Answer these questions, then present your idea to the class.

1 What's your structure?

2 Where will you build it? What materials will you use?

3 Why's it special? What makes it a wonder?

 THINK BIG What are more important, natural world wonders or man-made world wonders? Why?

31 Read the report. Then copy the idea web and use the information to complete it.

Australia is one of the seven continents but it's also a country. It's known as the smallest continent in the world. Do you know why it's called 'the land down under'? It's because Australia is located below the equator.

More than 22 million people live in Australia. Aborigines are the original inhabitants of Australia but people from many different countries have come to Australia to live. Today, most people in Australia speak English.

The capital of Australia is Canberra. Other big and important cities in Australia are Sydney, Melbourne, Brisbane and Perth.

Location and People ?

Capital ?

Country ?

Language Spoken ?

Major Cities ?

32 Choose a country to write a report about. Do research to find out facts about the country. Write them in an idea web.

33 Use your idea web to write your report. Share it with the class.

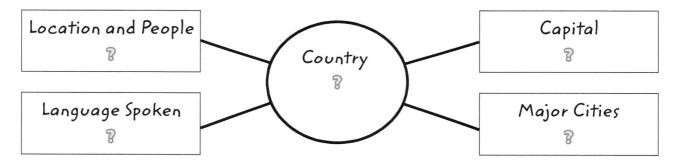

THINK BIG What makes you feel 'connected' to your home town/city?
Think in terms of:
- places you like
- memories
- people

34 Look at this list of features. Has your town or city (or a nearby town or city) got any of these? Copy the list and write the names and locations. Add any additional attractions to your list.

- a statue of a famous person or historical event
- an art museum
- a history, anthropological or science museum
- a concert hall or event centre
- a stadium or athletic field
- old houses or other historical structures
- religious places that are historically or culturally important
- a beautiful park or garden
- a famous restaurant
- a college or university

PROJECT

The Clock Tower in Chetbury was built in 1870. It used to be a village hall and a fire station. Today, it's a historic building with shops in it.

35 Work in a small group. Prepare a map for a bicycle trip to six famous or interesting places in your town/city, county or country.

1 See pages 138 and 139 for ideas.

2 Make a map.

3 Prepare a brief oral presentation of your map. Make notes on index cards. List information like this about each place:
   - the location
   - a short description of the place
   - when the place was built
   - why it was built

4 Tell your classmates about each place as you share your map with them.

36 **Listen, read and repeat.**

1 able   **2** ful   **3** ly

 37 **Listen and blend the sounds.**

1 c-o-m-f-or-t-able   comfortable   **2** p-ea-ce-ful   peaceful

3 d-ee-p-ly   deeply   **4** w-a-sh-able   washable

5 b-eau-t-i-ful   beautiful   **6** s-l-ow-ly   slowly

 38 **Listen and chant.**

> I feel so comfortable
> On my soft pillow.
> I breathe deeply.
> I breathe slowly
> And I have a peaceful sleep.

39 **Work in a small group. Play a guessing game.**

A Use the words and phrases from the boxes to create a list of clues for a guessing game.

> cathedral   city   island   mausoleum   monument   place   statue   temple   tower

> is a/an   is famous for / located in

B Take turns giving clues to your group. Keep giving information until someone in your group guesses correctly.

This is an island that's famous for giant rocks.

No, not Stonehenge. Stonehenge isn't an island. The giant rocks are statues.

Correct!

I'm not sure. Stonehenge?

I know! It's Easter Island.

40 Complete each sentence with a word from the box.

> mausoleum   pyramids   Statue   temple

1 The ❓ are burial places for ancient Egyptian pharaohs.

2 Borobudur in Indonesia is a famous Buddhist ❓ dedicated to Buddha.

3 The ❓ of Liberty was given to the United States by the people of France.

4 The Taj Mahal is actually a ❓ where Mumtaz Mahal is buried.

41 Combine the pairs of sentences into one. Use who or that.

1 Machu Picchu is an ancient city. It is 2,430 metres above sea level in the Andes Mountains. ❓

2 The *moai* are giant rock statues. They were found on Easter Island. ❓

3 Christ the Redeemer is a famous statue. It stands over the city of Rio de Janeiro. ❓

4 Michelangelo was an Italian Renaissance artist. He created the statue known as *David*. ❓

5 The Great Sphinx is a monument. It has remained a mystery to this day. ❓

6 Johan Vermeer was a Dutch painter. He painted *Girl with a Pearl Earring* in 1665. ❓

42 Read and rewrite the sentences.

1 English is spoken by most people in Australia.
Most people in Australia speak English.

2 The Great Pyramids were built by Egyptians. ❓

3 DNA of old bones was used by scientists. ❓

4 Dimitri has his dog fed by his neighbour every day. ❓

5 Mum had breakfast prepared by Matilda. ❓

I Can

- **talk about famous places and structures around the world.**

- **describe places and structures using the passive voice, relative clauses and the causative form.**

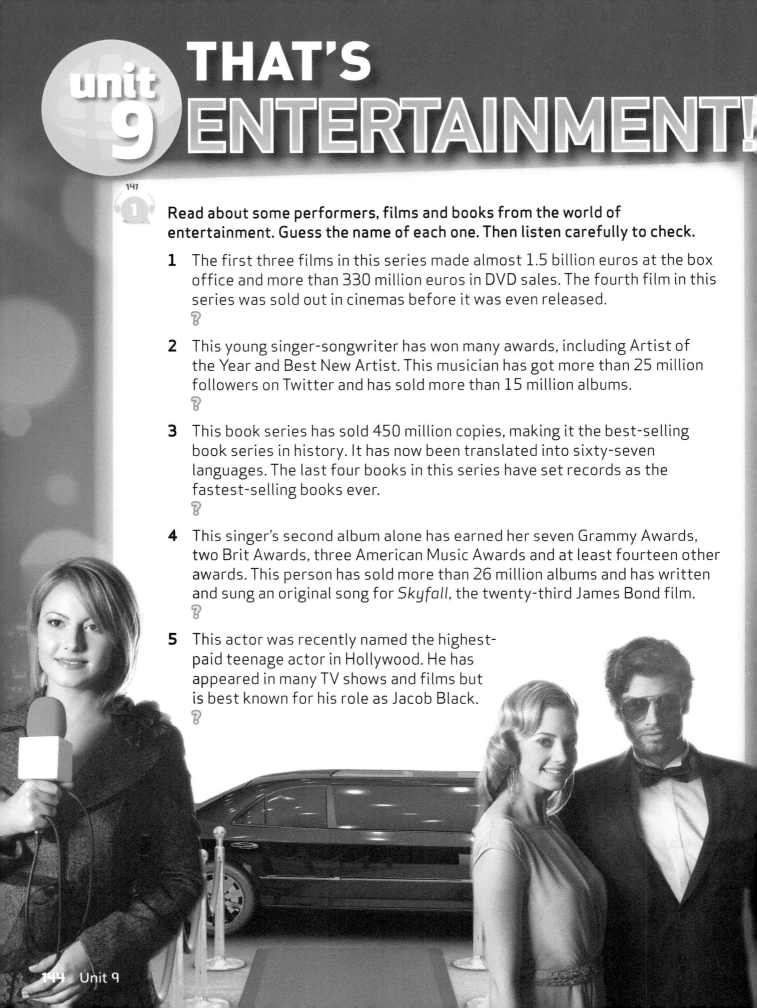

unit 9 THAT'S ENTERTAINMENT!

1 Read about some performers, films and books from the world of entertainment. Guess the name of each one. Then listen carefully to check.

1 The first three films in this series made almost 1.5 billion euros at the box office and more than 330 million euros in DVD sales. The fourth film in this series was sold out in cinemas before it was even released.

2 This young singer-songwriter has won many awards, including Artist of the Year and Best New Artist. This musician has got more than 25 million followers on Twitter and has sold more than 15 million albums.

3 This book series has sold 450 million copies, making it the best-selling book series in history. It has now been translated into sixty-seven languages. The last four books in this series have set records as the fastest-selling books ever.

4 This singer's second album alone has earned her seven Grammy Awards, two Brit Awards, three American Music Awards and at least fourteen other awards. This person has sold more than 26 million albums and has written and sung an original song for *Skyfall*, the twenty-third James Bond film.

5 This actor was recently named the highest-paid teenage actor in Hollywood. He has appeared in many TV shows and films but is best known for his role as Jacob Black.

2 Listen. Copy the diary into your notebook and complete it with the things that Becky has planned to do. Use names of events from the box. Then match the events to the pictures below.

> book signing   comic book exhibition   concert   festival   film premiere

January ?

February ?

March ?

April ?

May ?

1   ?

2   ?

3   ?

4   ?

5   ?

3 Work with a partner. Talk about Becky's activities for next year and what she said she was going to do each month.

What did Becky say she was doing in January?

She said she was going to an Adele concert.

THINK BIG What do you consider good entertainment. Why?

 **143**

4 Listen and read. Which reviewer hopes Stanley's third album will be better than his second?

www.reviewsbykids.com

▶ TV Shows
▶ Films
▶ Books
▶ Clothes
▼ Music
  • mp3
  • Best Sellers
  • Today's Deals
  • CDs

CUSTOMER REVIEWS
You Know It!

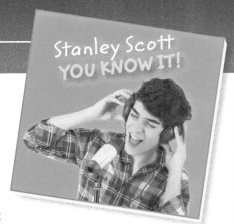

Stanley Scott
YOU KNOW IT!

5 stars: ★ ★ ★ ★ ★ 139 reviews
4 stars: ★ ★ ★ ★ ☆ 82 reviews
3 stars: ★ ★ ★ ☆ ☆ 17 reviews
2 stars: ★ ★ ☆ ☆ ☆ 2 reviews
1 star: ★ ☆ ☆ ☆ ☆ 7 reviews

Display reviews by most helpful:

★ ★ ★ ★ ★ **Love it! Love it! Love it!**
by Little_Kitty
I really liked Stanley's first album but I didn't know what to expect with the second one. My best friend said this album was even better than the first one and he was so right! There's a rumour that it's going to be nominated for the Best Album Award. How cool is that!

★ ★ ★ ★ ★ **This was so worth the wait!**
by music_lover_2003
I am a huge Stanley fan. I have been waiting for this album for SO LONG and it's finally HERE! My friends and I bought it as soon as it came out. I'm going to a concert of his next week. I can't wait!

★ ★ ★ ★ ☆ **Not as good as the first one but still really good.**
by JJ_keyboards
Scott's first album was pretty good. Everybody could see that this guy had a lot of talent but then the recording companies started to control Scott and his music. The sound in the new album isn't as good as it was in the first. I still like Scott's music a lot so I bought the new album. But I'm hoping that he'll go back to his old sound when he makes his third album!

★ ★ ☆ ☆ ☆ **Not bad but a little disappointing.**

by star_fan

I bought Stanley Scott's first album and I really liked it. My friend told me that Stanley had been working with my favourite singer, Sasha Littleton, so I thought maybe the music in this album would be different from the first one. Well, it's OK but I was a little disappointed. I'm still going to see him at Fairlop festival next month and hope he'll play most of his old songs.

★ ☆ ☆ ☆ ☆ **AWFUL!**

by music_for_life

I think this kid has got some talent but this is NOT music! It's the product of a big recording company. It's their sound, not Stanley Scott's. The lyrics, the music, everything is so boring. I'm not going to buy his next one if it's like this. There's no creativity in this album at all! Even kids like me know the difference between real music and stuff like this.

READING COMPREHENSION

5 Match the two parts to create a summary of each of the five reviews.

1 Little_Kitty said…

2 Music_lover_2003 said…

3 JJ_keyboards said that…

4 Star_fan said…

5 Music_for_life said that…

a there was no creativity in Stanley's second album.

b Stanley's album was going to be nominated for an award.

c Stanley's second album wasn't as good as his first.

d he was going to see Stanley at a festival next month.

e she was going to see Stanley perform next week.

 THINK BIG What did most people who reviewed Stanley's second album think of it? Where do you usually see music and film reviews? Why do people write reviews? Why do you think people read them?

Language in Action

145

6 Listen and read. What did Darren's mum say?

Carol: What are you doing?

Darren: I'm counting the money that I've saved up from my pocket money.

Carol: Here, let me help. So what are you going to spend this on?

Darren: I want to go to the comic book exhibition. Hannah's dad is taking her and Mum said that I could go with them. But I've got to buy the ticket myself.

Carol: Why do you want to spend all your money on that?

Darren: Because I love comic books! And I've never been to a comic book exhibition before.

Carol: Laura said she was going, too, so there will be three of you there.

Darren: Great! It's going to be brilliant. There's an art competition and I'm entering my comic book.

Carol: Good idea. You're great at drawing.

7 Practise the dialogue in 6 with a partner.

146

8 Listen and match. Then complete the sentences using the correct words from the box.

> fantastic   good
> impressive   stunning

1 A reviewer said the animation was ?.   **2** Luke said it was really ?.

3 A boy said it was ?.   **4** Her friend said it was ?.

a

b

c

d

Direct speech	Reported speech
Claire said, "The album **isn't** as good as the last one."	Claire said (that) the album **wasn't** as good as the last one.
Josh said, "I**'m going** to the premiere."	Josh said (that) he **was going** to the premiere.

Tip: Change the verb in the reported statement from the present simple to the past simple or from the present continuous to the past continuous.

9 Read what each person is saying. Rewrite their words in your notebook as reported speech.

1 Adele is my favourite singer.

Alana

2 I like One Direction better than Adele.

Mike

3 My parents are going to the opera.

Shari

10 Change the direct speech to reported speech.

1 My mum said, "His concerts are expensive."

2 Julia said, "The new vampire film is getting bad reviews."

3 Rosie said, "I'm going to win the competition."

4 Alex said, "There are only a few tickets left."

5 James said, "I'm reading a great book at the moment."

6 Harry said, "The concert starts at 8."

7 Emma said, "Dad's coming to pick me up after the festival".

8 George said, "Her new album is much better than her last one".

11 Ask and answer with a partner. Collect information with your class.

1 Do you like playing video or computer games?

2 Where/How do you play them? (on a computer, PlayStation®, Nintendo®, tablet, etc.)

3 How much time do you spend playing video games every week?

149
12 Listen and read. How did *Tetris*® become popular?

CONTENT WORDS

arcade game   artificial intelligence   coins   compete   gamer
games console   industry   intended   invent   multiplayer   shortage

---

The History of VIDEO GAMES

1   Have you ever heard of *Pong*®, *Pac-Man*® or Game Boy®? Believe it or not, these things were once as popular as *Nintendo*® and *PlayStation*®! Just fifty years ago, video games were very different. They were simply interactive computer programmes with an electronic display. They weren't even intended for entertainment. They were just experiments in artificial intelligence.

2   Nevertheless, a number of different video games were invented in the USA between 1950 and 1970. William Higinbotham, a physicist, invented a game called *Tennis for Two* in 1958. It was popular and people could play it in a computer laboratory but it was never sold in shops. Then in 1962, students at Massachusetts Institute of Technology (MIT) created *Spacewar!* It was still too expensive to run on a home computer but it was sent to university laboratories all over the USA, inspiring students to develop other computer games.

1952–1970

3   In 1972, an arcade table tennis game called *Pong*® was invented. It was very popular and many people wanted to play it in their living rooms but it was still too big and expensive. They had to wait three years for a home version! Then, in 1978, the Japanese company *Nintendo*® invented *Space Invaders*. People could play it in machines that worked with coins. *Space Invaders* was the first ever video game to track and display high scores… and its popularity in Japan caused a national shortage of coins! Later, game developers developed multiplayer games, allowing people to compete at home. At last, people could use games consoles and play games on TV.

1972–1978

4   In 1989, *Game Boy*® arrived in shops. This black and white Japanese video game player became popular with the puzzle game *Tetris*®. People all over the world were now playing games at home. The computer gaming industry was changing by the day and more and more money was being spent on high technology, realistic games.

1989

5   By 2004, people were using the *Wii*™. It was a big hit because people could play with their whole body! Games developers were looking for ways to get gamers out of their chairs and the *Wii*™ was their answer.

2004

6   In just fifty years, video games have reached an amazing quality. If games can change this much in such a short time, what will happen next?

13 Look at 12. What happened in these years? Take notes.

1958 ?   1962 ?   1972 ?
1978 ?   1989 ?   2004 ?

14 Look at 12. Read and say true or false.

1 Early computer games were developed for scientific research.

2 William Higinbotham was a student at MIT.

3 Computer programming students could play *Spacewar!* at universities.

4 People didn't play computer games at home because they didn't want to.

5 *Space Invaders* first became popular in the USA.

6 In 1989, games developers were trying to make games more real.

7 With the *Wii*™, computer gamers became more active.

15 Read the statements. Do they say positive (P) or negative (N) things about playing video games?

1 Video games teach me to find solutions to problems.

2 When we're playing a video game in English, we have to understand the language or we can't continue.

3 When I come home and play video games, I spend less time on my homework.

4 Some video games make people more violent.

5 I prefer playing video games to playing outside.

6 Some games are about organising your life and your money. They're really good.

7 I love playing video games because I can forget about everything else.

8 It's great to know about video games because designing games would be a brilliant job.

16 Look at 15. Which statements do you agree or disagree with? Why? Organise a class vote.

17 Find out about a video game you like. Who invented it? When was it invented? What do you have to do in the game? Why do you like it? Write a paragraph in your notebook.

• • • • • • • • • • (THE FUTURE) ▶

18 Listen and read. What's Grandma's best friend called? When did she meet her?

Scott: Grandma, what was your first day at school like? How did you feel?

Grandma: School? I was a bit frightened of the big school but I didn't want to show it. My mum told me to be good and my dad told me not to talk in lessons.

Scott: What about your brother? Did he give you any advice?

Grandma: Yes, he did. He told me not to eat sweets at school!

Scott: Was your teacher strict?

Grandma: Yes, she was. She told us to be quiet and listen to her or she'd tell the headmaster!

Scott: Did you make any friends on your first day?

Grandma: I did! A girl called Amy asked me to play hopscotch with her at break.

Scott: And did you?

Grandma: Yes, I did. That was sixty years ago and Amy and I are still friends. And we still play hopscotch when nobody's watching!

19 Look at 18 and complete.

Mum: "Be good."	My mum **told me** ¹ .
Dad: "Don't talk in lessons."	My dad **told me** ² in lessons.
Brother: "Don't eat sweets at school."	My brother **told me** ³ at school.
Teacher: "Be quiet and listen to me."	The teacher **told** ⁴ **to** be quiet and listen to ⁵ .
Amy: "Please play hopscotch with me."	Amy **asked me** ⁶ .

20 Match the sentences to make the story of Cinderella.

1 The ugly sisters told

2 The fairy godmother told

3 At the ball, the prince asked Cinderella

4 The prince asked all the women in the land

5 In the end, the prince asked Cinderella

a Cinderella to leave the ball before midnight.

b to dance with him.

c to marry him.

d Cinderella to wash their clothes.

e to try on the glass slipper.

21 Look at 20. What did the people say? Which words change?

The ugly sisters: "Wash our clothes!"

22 Who told Beth to do these things? Match the people and make the indirect commands.

> the dentist the doctor the lifeguard the photographer the teacher the zookeeper

1 "Don't run around the pool."
The lifeguard told Beth not to run around the pool.

2 "Don't chew gum at school."

3 "Take this medicine three times a day."

4 "Look at the camera and smile, please."

5 "Open your mouth, please."

6 "Don't feed the animals."

23 Match the sentence beginnings to the commands. Then complete sentences 1–6 in your notebook. Follow the example

1 I was really hungry, so I told ?   **a** Asya, can you get me a glass of water?

2 It was a dangerous road, so I asked ?   **b** Kemal, don't eat my crisps.

3 I felt ill, so I asked ?   **c** Justin, don't waste my time.

4 I was late for school, so I asked ?   **d** Leo, can you lend me your mobile?

5 My phone was broken, so I asked ?   **e** Selda, don't drive so fast.

6 I was angry, so I told ?   **f** Mum, can you give me a lift?

24 Complete these sentences for you. What did you say?

1 It was very hot in the classroom, so I asked/told ?

2 It was a secret, so I asked/told ?

3 I couldn't do my homework, so I asked/told ?

4 It was fantastic music, so I asked/told ?

Unique Musical Instruments

1   Music is as old as mankind. It's a form of communication and, just like language, many instruments are unique to a specific culture or area. This article takes a look at just a few of the instruments that we associate with different countries and their history.

2   **Bagpipes** are very old, although we don't know exactly how old because they aren't built to last a long time. Bagpipes consist of a bag (which was traditionally made of sheep's stomach) and pipes. Most people think of Scotland when they think of bagpipes, but bagpipes are also used traditionally in other parts of Europe.

3   The **sitar** is a stringed instrument used in classical Indian music. It's common in India, Pakistan and Bangladesh. It was probably developed from a similar Persian instrument in about the 18th century. A sitar looks quite similar to a guitar but its sound is very different. It makes Indian styles of music very distinctive.

25   **Look at the instruments and the countries. Which instruments and countries can you match? Discuss with a partner.**

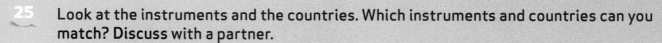

alpine horn   bandoneon   the bagpipes   sitar   steel drums

Argentina   India   Scotland   Switzerland   Trinidad and Tobago

I think the steel drums are common in India.

I don't think so. I remember that our music teacher said that they were common in Trinidad.

26   **Read the article quickly. Which instruments in 25 does it mention? Check your guesses about the countries they're from.**

4 The **Steel drums** were first used in the 1700s. These drums were originally created out of oil drums to celebrate Carnival in Trinidad and Tobago, but their popularity is growing around the world. The steel is bent to create a distinctive sound and a number of different notes. Many musicians play six to eight drums at a time.

5 The **alpine horn** is associated with herdsmen, especially people living in mountainous regions. Originally, Swiss farmers used alpine horns to communicate with each other across the mountains, but historians believe the horn was also used as many as 2,000 years ago by Celtic people. Most alpine horns (also called alphorns) are carved out of spruce wood and they've got a mellow, echoey sound. Some famous composers such as Mozart and Bach also wrote music for this instrument.

6 The **bandoneon** is a type of concertina. Although it was invented in Germany in 1846 to play church music, it has become the symbol of Argentine tango. Astor Piazzolla, the famous Argentine composer and musician, made the instrument world-famous in the 20th century with his tango compositions. The instrument itself is extremely complex and difficult to play, as each button makes a different note when played pushing in and pushing out.

7 These are just some of the unusual instruments that are part of different cultures. Which instruments is your country famous for?

27 **Listen and read. Then say** true **or** false.

1 Musicians can play two to four drums at the same time.

2 The bagpipes are a modern musical instrument.

3 The alpine horn wasn't used for sending messages.

4 The steel drums are played during a famous period of celebrations.

5 The bandoneon requires great skill.

28 **Look at the questions. Interview three people in your class. Take notes and share the results with your class.**

1 Do you play a musical instrument? How long have you been playing it for?

2 Which instrument would you like to learn how to play? Why?

3 What's your favourite kind of music? Which instruments are used to play it?

THINK BIG **Is there a traditional kind of music in your country, such as folk music? What is it? Which instruments do the musicians use?**

29 Read the film review. What does the reviewer say about the story, the acting and the special effects? Discuss with a partner.

www.filmreviews.com

FILM REVIEW

Don't Miss *Solar Scare*!
by Ron Whitmore

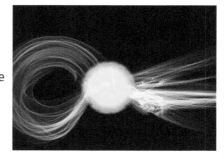

Solar Scare is a sci-fi thriller. The story is based on the idea that the sun has got the ability to think and feel. The sun has become angry with Earth because people are planning to build colonies in space. The sun shoots out huge flares of fire that get bigger each day. Scientists are afraid that soon the deadly flares will reach Earth.

John Medias plays the hero of the story. His character is determined to find a way to build a bubble around Earth to protect it from the sun. At first he thinks he can't do it but then he meets a scientist, played by Martina DeNovo. She has been working on a secret plan to build a bubble herself but spies from another country have been trying to steal her plans.

Both actors play their roles convincingly. Their acting is quite good and the story grabs the audience from the beginning. But the best thing about *Solar Scare* is the special effects. They're stunning! Go and see the film just for the special effects. They're worth the price of the ticket.

He said that the best thing was the special effects!

Cool! I'll check it out this weekend.

30 Follow these steps to write your own film review. It can be positive or negative.

1 Choose a film you have seen recently. Describe what type of film it is.

2 Briefly describe the story.

3 What did you think about the story, the acting and other features?

4 Write notes.

5 Use your notes to write your review.

TIP

Try to use vivid adjectives as you write, for example: *stunning, captivating, tense, gripping,* etc.

31 Read a classmate's review. Report back to the class to share what your classmate said about the film.

32 Read the four different opinions. Match each opinion to an item in the box.

> **a** an exhibition
> **b** a concert (2x)
> **c** a video game

1 It was the best live musical performance I've ever seen.

2 The event, which was held in a dark hall, was badly organised and too busy for me!

3 It was the most exciting game I've ever played. I can't wait until they launch the sequel.

4 The music was much too loud. I won't be going to one again anytime soon.

PROJECT

33 Make an Opinion Map. **Work in a small group.**

1 Choose a film, book, comic book or album that everyone in your group knows.

2 Share your opinions about it.

3 Record what each person thinks about it on an Opinion Map.

4 Present your Opinion Map to the class:

We reviewed Lady Gaga's new album. Ali said it wasn't as good as her last one, etc.

Ali: It's not as good as her last one.

Kyle: It's great to listen to while I'm doing my homework!

Lady Gaga's New Album

Lisa: The music is too loud! It drowns out her voice.

Sam: The best! It's better than any of her other albums.

TIP

Show interest when people share their opinions. Here are some expressions:

I think so, too.   *Why do you say that?*
That's interesting.   *Really? I don't agree.*

 THINK BIG Why is it important to listen to different opinions? Think in terms of:
• respect   • having an open mind   • learning something new

34 Listen, read and repeat.

1 sion   **2** tion   **3** ation

35 Listen and blend the sounds.

1 t-e-l-e-v-i-sion   television   **2** f-i-c-tion   fiction

3 c-e-l-e-b-r-ation   celebration   **4** d-e-c-i-sion   decision

5 o-p-tion   option   **6** i-n-v-i-t-ation   invitation

36 Listen and chant.

I've got an invitation
To a birthday celebration.
We'll watch science fiction
Films on television.
Now that's a good decision!

37 Work with a partner. Copy and complete this chart for yourself. Then write your partner's answers.

What's your favourite... ?	Me	My partner
animated film		
action film		
comedy film		
comic book		
video game		
actor		
singer		
song		
album		

38 With your partner, talk about three of the items on the list. Why are those your favourites?

Krypton Kid is my favourite animated film. The animation is brilliant. The ending is amazing!

39 Complete each sentence with a word from the box.

> book signing   comic book exhibition   concert   festival   premiere   review

1 I wanted to go to the Ne-Yo ❓ last night but it was sold out. I read Gayle Smart's ❓ of it and she said it was amazing.

2 The Stamford Summer Brit-pop Music ❓ has been announced for June next year.

3 Do you like comic books? Have you ever been to a ❓?

4 Did you hear? *Flipped* is now a film! The ❓ is next week. And the author will be at a ❓ event at Bookspace on the same day.

40 Read the dialogue. Then answer the questions using reported speech.

Brian: What are you doing this weekend?

Carol: I'm going to a hip-hop festival. It starts tomorrow.

Brian: Don't go! I heard the weather will be very bad!

Carol: It's OK, the festival is in the City Hall.

Brian: Oh good. So, who's going to be at the festival?

Carol: Jessie J, Kelly Rowland, Diddy and plenty more.

Brian: It sounds amazing... I wish I could go.

1 What did Carol say she was doing this weekend?

2 What did Brian suggest that Carol shouldn't do?

3 What did Brian say about the festival when he heard who was going to be there?

41 Read and complete.

1 Mum: Give me your mobile phone.   My mum told me ❓.

2 Sister: Don't take my books.   My sister told me ❓.

3 Friend: Can you help me?   My friend asked me ❓.

I Can

- **talk about entertainment.**
- **talk about people's opinions.**
- **report what people say.**

How Well Do I Know It? Can I Use It?

1 Think about it. Read and draw. Practise.

😊 I know this.   😐 I need more practice.   😟 I don't know this.

	PAGES			
Mysteries: Atlantis, Bermuda Triangle, crop circles… **Mystery-related words:** phenomenon, unsolved, proof…	112–113	😊	😐	😟
Structures: palace, statue, tower… **Famous places:** Statue of Liberty, Taj Mahal…	128–129	😊	😐	😟
Entertainment: concert, film premiere, book signing…	145	😊	😐	😟
The Sailing Stones **are** in California, **aren't** they? The aurora borealis **isn't** a real mystery, **is** it? We **can't** see crop circles from the ground, **can** we?	116–117	😊	😐	😟
a **short-sleeved** shirt, feel **half-asleep**, be **well-known**… - Paul's tired. - **So am** I! **So is** Pam! - I didn't like it. - **Neither did** Kate!	120–121	😊	😐	😟
The Taj Mahal **is visited** by millions of tourists each year. Machu Picchu **was discovered** in 1911 (by archaeologists).	132–133	😊	😐	😟
Leonardo da Vinci was the famous artist and inventor **who** painted the *Mona Lisa*. The Eiffel Tower is a landmark **that** has become the symbol of Paris, France.	132–133	😊	😐	😟
Jack **had his photo taken** yesterday. I need to **have my hair cut**. I'll **get it done** tomorrow.	136–137	😊	😐	😟
Claire said, "The album **isn't** as good as the last one." She said the album **wasn't** as good as the last one.	148–149	😊	😐	😟
Mum said, "Be quiet! Please don't disturb me!" Mum **told us to be quiet**. She **asked us not to disturb her**.	152–153	😊	😐	😟

I Can Do It!

157

2 **Get ready.**

A Choose the correct word or phrase to complete the dialogue. Then listen and check.

Kevin: This film is boring. I don't want to watch the end.

Tina: (So do / Neither do) I. Hey, do you want to watch *Mystery Tour*?

Kevin: I don't know. What's it about?

Tina: It's a new programme about scientists (who / who's) travel around the world and study mysterious places like the Bermuda Triangle.

Kevin: Oh, I've heard about that! My friend at school said it (was / were) really good.

Tina: Oops, wait a minute, Kevin. It's not on until 9:00. Your mum told you (will be / to be) in bed by 8:30, didn't she?

Kevin: That's during the week. On Saturdays, I'm allowed to stay up until 9:30.

Tina: Oh, lucky you. You can watch it, then.

Kevin: Mystery Tour is scary, (isn't / doesn't) it?

Tina: No. It isn't really scary. It's (make / made) for people (who's / that) like science. You're good at science, (are / aren't) you?

Kevin: Yes, I am. Hey, do you know *Dark Corners*?

Tina: *Dark Corners*! Now that's a scary programme!

Kevin: It was my favourite programme but it (is dropped / was dropped) last month.

Tina: Probably because it was too scary!

B Practise the dialogue in **A** with a partner.

C Ask and answer the questions with a partner.

1 What is the TV programme *Mystery Tour* about?

2 What has Kevin heard about the programme?

3 Will Kevin be able to watch the programme with Tina? Why/Why not?

4 Does the programme sound interesting to you? Why/Why not?

Get set.

 STEP 1 Cut out the cards on page 163 of your Activity Book.

 STEP 2 Assign a group leader. The group leader gets a set of yellow cards, the group gets a set of green cards and each group member gets a set of orange cards. Now you're ready to **Go!**

 Go!

A Work in a group of five.

- The group leader takes the yellow card. Each other member takes one of the green cards. As the leader reads each yellow card, the pupil with the green card that correctly completes the description reads it.

- For each title, group members turn over orange cards and describe what 'your best friend' says about the title.

B Count the positive and negative reviews for each title and decide which ones your group is going to check out. Report to the class.

5 Write about yourself in your notebook.

- What famous place would you like to visit? Why?
- Talk about a film/show/album/game that a friend has recommended to you. What did he/she say about it?
- What do your mum and dad often ask or tell you to do? Do you always do it?
- Where do you get your hair cut? What about the other people in your family?

All About Me

Date:_____

_____

_____

How Well Do I Know It Now?

6 Look at page 160 and your notebook. Draw again.

A Use a different colour.

B Read and think.

I can ask my teacher for help.

I can practise.

7 Rate this Checkpoint.

 very easy   easy   hard   very hard   fun   OK   not fun

Units 7-9 Exam Preparation

- Part A -

158

Listen and look at the picture. There is one example.

Look at the picture and read the story. Write words to complete the sentences about the story. You can use 1, 2, 3 or 4 words.

Our comic book adventure

My name is Michael and Betty is my older sister. We both love comic books and we often play video games together. Last Saturday, my parents took us to a comic book exhibition in a town near us. We were both very excited about that! When we got to the exhibition, we saw that our favourite author was doing a book signing. Cool! My mum agreed to buy his new book for Betty and said that I could read it, too. I said that was a great idea! We got the book signed right away!

On our way home in the car after the exhibition, Mum decided to stop and sit by the river. Betty said she was going to read her new book. Unfortunately, five minutes later, we heard her shouting for help! She'd dropped the book into the river and it was gone! We were so sad but then Mum had a good idea. She had the email address of the author, so she emailed him when we got home and told him the story. "No problem!" he answered. He said he would send another signed copy of the book the next day. Mum thanked him very much and said that we were very lucky people!

Examples

Michael and Betty are brother and _____ *sister* _____ .

One of their favourite hobbies is playing _____ *video games* _____ .

Questions

1 Michael's family went to a _____ exhibition last Saturday.

2 At the exhibition, their _____ was signing books and they bought one.

3 After the exhibition, Mum wanted to sit _____ .

4 Betty had an accident and _____ into the river.

5 Fortunately, Mum had the author's _____ so she could send him a message.

Wordlist

Find these words in your language. Then write in your notebook.

Unit 1	Page	Unit 2	Page	Unit 3	Page
assignment	8	ability	26	acceptable	42
average	10	accomplishment	35	according to	42
belief	10	ages	26	based on	42
be more careful	5	become a doctor	20	be upset with	37
break	10	Braille	26	character	42
bright	10	climb a mountain	21	(cheat/don't cheat)	
ceremony	10	co-found	26	in a test	36
composting	15	compose	26	common sense	48
curriculum	15	conflict resolution	32	consequences	47
do homework	4	critical thinking	32	ethical	42
do it earlier	5	determined	26	ethical behaviour	42
do it again	5	exceptional talent	26	ethics	42
end up	6	gifted	26	excuse	42
focused	15	inspiration	26	feel good about	
free time	10	inventor	24	(himself/herself)	37
gather	10	keep in touch	26	feel guilty	36
hand in (an essay)	5	journalist	31	get into trouble	36
homeschooling	7	leader	31	harmless	42
licence	8	legend	26	hasty	47
limited	10	meet a world leader	20	morally	42
memorising	15	neutral environment	32	pass on	47
pace	14	opera	26	perspective	42
packed	10	peace	31	proverb	47
pay attention to the time	5	social media	26	qualities	42
period	10	speak another language	20	reap	47
practical	14	start a company	20	regret	47
quality time	16	symphony	26	respectful	42
strengthen	10	write and publish a book	20	(return/don't return)	
stressful	6			a wallet	37
study for a test	5			sayings	47
study period	10			sound advice	47
timetable	4			sow	47
typical	10			(tell/don't tell) the truth	39
workshop	14			traits	42
				treat	42
				weigh up	47

Wordlist

Base Form	Past Simple	Base Form	Past Simple
become	became	meet	met
blame	blamed	pass	passed
bring	brought	pay	paid
cheat	cheated	play	played
climb	climbed	publish	published
compete	competed	read	read
cultivate	cultivated	regret	regretted
deceive	deceived	return	returned
digest	digested	run	ran
do	did	speak	spoke
download	downloaded	start	started
earn	earnt	study	studied
estimate	estimated	tell	told
feel	felt	travel	travelled
finish	finished	treat	treated
fly	flew	turn	turned
get	got	tweet	tweeted
give	gave	upload	uploaded
hand	handed	win	won
have	had	work	worked
influence	influenced	write	wrote

Pearson Education Limited
Edinburgh Gate
Harlow
Essex CM20 2JE
England
and Associated Companies throughout the world.

www.pearsonelt.com/bigenglish

© Pearson Education Limited 2015

Authorised adaptation from the United States edition entitled Big English, 1st Edition, by Mario Herrera and Christopher Sol Cruz. Published by Pearson Education Inc. © 2013 by Pearson Education, Inc.

The right of Mario Herrera and Christopher Sol Cruz to be identified as the authors of this Work have been asserted by them in accordance with the Copyright, Designs and Patents Act 1988.

First published 2015

Fifteenth impression 2022

ISBN: 978-1-4479-9469-5

Set in Apex Sans
Editorial and design management by hyphen S.A.
Printed by CPI Group (UK) Ltd, Croydon CR0 4YY

Acknowledgements

The publisher would like to thank the following for their kind permission to reproduce photographs:

(Key: b-bottom; c-centre; l-left; r-right; t-top)

123RF.com: Alan Finlayson 135b, Andres Rodriguez 152, Boy Sitti 28, Chris Elwell 44, chris willemsen 154cl, cycloneproject 65, elnavegante 155b, Ksenia Ragozina 96br, Shi Jinshou 135t, Tono Balaguer 98; **Alamy Images:** Ace Stock Limited 78, Aflo Foto Agency 26b, Allstar Picture Library 159, Anders Blomqvist 69 (Rajeesh), Andrew Woodley 154tr, Big Cheese Photo LLC 91t, Blend Images 35/1, 69 (Kat), blickwinkel 114t, Cultura RM 33br, 35/3, david pearson 122-123, Design Pics Inc 4, dieKleinert 113/2, Edd Westmacott 145/3, eddie linssen 33t, Fredrick Kippe 144br, geogphotos 74t, 106c, GL Archive 26tl, Glow Asia RF 6/1, 7/3, 69 (Shen), 104l, 129br, Hemis 113/1, Ilya Genkin 128/5, Image Source 32, Image Source Plus 91br, INTERFOTO 150t, Jamie Pham Photography 145/2, Jeff Morgan 14 145/1, JHPhoto 150b, Marc Romanelli 132, Megapress 69 (Anashe), michel platini Fernandes Borges 6/4, Mikko Mattila 15, OJO Images Ltd 40, 148, PhotoAlto sas 6/6, RGB Ventures LLC dba SuperStock 26tr, RubberBall 37 (lamp), Sabena Jane Blackbird 122t, 160t, Science Photo Library 156t; **Corbis:** Image Source 94, Randy Faris 90t; **DK Images:** Linda Whitwam 112t; **Fotolia.com:** ALCE 130, 131, AlienCat 112-113, amfroey01 23, Andres Rodriguez 60t, arekmalang 35/4, 52c, biker3 6/2, Boggy 100-101, bst2012 37 (Al), caminoel 128 (background), chawalitpix 80t, 106t, DragonImages 73, ecco 129 (background), Elenathewise 29, 35t, Eric Isselée 96t, faizzaki 96bl, feferoni 113/3, Felix Mizioznikov 36r, 52t, Forewer 157, gavran333 37 (necklace), grafikplusfoto 20tr, gui yong nian, hansenn 136, Iva 128/1, J_Foto 37 (wallet), Jörg Hackemann 87, 125b, Kalim 35/2, KaYann 128/4, lunamarina 88r, Marta 20-21 (background), Monteleone 7/4, PiLensPhoto 113/4, 160br, pumpchn 13, S.White 68, Sabphoto 20br, sellingpix 59t, sjhuls 141b, Subbotina Anna 129/6, vilainecrevette 105b, wenani 36-37; **Getty Images:** Michael Wells 114-115 (background), Sheldon Levis / Photolibrary 61, TAO Images Limited 33bl, Vittorio Ricci - Italy / Flickr 114c, WireImage / Barry King 21 (below centre); **Glow Images:** 118b, Eckhard Eibner 155t, Perspectives 20cr; **Newscom:** Lucas Oleniuk 21 (above centre), Ma Yan / Xinhua / Photoshot 21t; **Pearson Education:** Christopher Sol Cruz 22; **Pearson Education Ltd:** Studio 8 82, 120, Gareth Boden 12; **Press Association Images:** Robert F. Bukaty 30-31; **Rex Features:** View Pictures 60b; **Shutterstock.com:** 129/3, Aleksandar Todorovic 128/2, Ann Worthy 75br, 145br, Anna Omelchenko 145/4, 160 (above centre), antipathique 74 (background), AVAVA 59br, 90b, bikeriderlondon 88l, 149/1, CandyBox Images 14, chungking 128/3, claudia veja 144bl, Costazzurra 74b, CREATISTA 75tc, Danomyte 86, Dieter Hawlan 101c, 154tl, Dudarev Mikhail 134-135 (background), Edyta Pawlowska 36l, egd 145/5, erashov 149/2, fotohunter 138l, Galina Barskaya 5tr, Gelpi JM 75c, Gurgen Bakhshetsyan 143, holbox 37 (Angela), Hubis 64, Hugo Felix 146, Hurst Photo 49, ievgen sosnytskyi 95, Intellistudies 63, irin-k 46-47 (background), Jaimie Duplass 11l, 21bl, 142r, James Steidl 144bc, JaySi 79, John David Bigl III 105t, jsouthby 149/3, julia 134, 160bl, Julian Rovagnati 17, Kamira 100l, karelnoppe 80b, Kirill Saveliev 140, 160 (below centre), Kiselev Andrey Valerevich 5b, kouptsova 6/3, 11r, 21br, 37br, 71tr, 126r, 154br, Lisa F. Young 116, Magdanatka 118 (background), Matthew Jacques 128/6, michaeljung 91bl, milias1987 42, Miriam Doerr 154cr, Monkey Business Images 24, 59bl, 71tl, 90c, 156b, Nella 129/1, Neo Edmund 46-47, Nestor Noci 129/5, Odua Images 71b, Oleg_Mit 72, Oleksiy Mark 58, 106b, Pamela Mullins 75cl, Pete Pahham 25, photogl 20l, 52b, pippa west 138r,

Pius Lee 129/4, R. Gino Santa Maria 5tl, 7/1, 158, Real Deal Photo 75tr, Rob Byron 37bl, Robert Crum 37 (Emily), Ruslan Guzov 129bl, S-F 74c, Sanmongkhol 126l, 154bl, Shane W Thompson 101r, Slazdi 141t, Somchai Som 129/2, 160bc, Syda Productions 75bl, 113bl, 145bl, szefei 127, Tara Flake 6/5, 7/2, 104r, Tracy Whiteside 75tl, 75cr, 113br, upthebanner 133, wizdata 10, wow 125t, Zurijeta 71cl, 142l; **SuperStock:** SOMOS 8

Cover images: *Front:* **Corbis:** Tetra Images / Rob Lewine r; **Shutterstock.com:** Kamira l, Pi-Lens

All other images © Pearson Education

Every effort has been made to trace the copyright holders and we apologise in advance for any unintentional omissions. We would be pleased to insert the appropriate acknowledgement in any subsequent edition of this publication.

Illustrated by
Valentina Belloni, Paula Franco, Anthony Lewis, Zaharias Papadopoulos (hyphen), Rob Sharp, Christos Skaltsas (hyphen)